UNDERSTANDING AND MANAGING DEPRESSION AND STRESS

JOSEPHINE SPIRE

Emerald Guides

© First Edition Josephine Spire 2017

978-1-84716-685-2

Printed by 4edge www.4edge.co.uk

Cover design by Bookworks Islington

Acknowledgements

I would like to convey my thanks to Jane, Jessica, Joseph, Dr John, Dr Jimmy, Dr Julius, Jofrey, Jerome for their tremendous and consistent support. A special gratitude also goes to Roger Sproston and the team at Emerald and all the people who greatly assisted me with my research throughout the course of writing this book. A big thank you to you all.

Introduction

Depression is a traumatic and cruel illness to suffer from, it can affect anyone regardless of their age, gender, race or status. The list of famous and successful men and women who have suffered from depression is drawn out.

Depression is a common illness which affects 150 million people worldwide. The majority of people when depressed describe their feelings as despondent, almost like being under a constant dark cloud encompassed by a lot of sadness, irritability, frustration, negativity and hopelessness among other symptoms, causing immense distress to the sufferer and their loved ones.

Depression is like any other illness, it has to be dealt with and not ignored, the sooner the better. You should understand that depression has no link to being weak or failing, it is an illness. Severe depression can be serious and life threatening and should be reported and treated immediately. If you are having suicidal thoughts, call your doctor and get help as soon as possible..

The good news is that many people who seek help for depression recover from it and turn their lives around positively. Relatively, stress affects our minds, bodies and relations. Most of us encounter stressful experiences in our lives but the difference is that we cope differently. Some people are better at dealing with their stress whereas other people find it a struggle to navigate through it. When we are under stress we go into 'fight' or 'flight' mode depending on how bad the situation is, this is the body's way of dealing with stress. Stress can be good or bad.

Good stress is that one that fires you on to achieve your goals, reach targets or improve your performance levels, bad stress is the stress that threatens your well-being mentally and physically to the point that you find daily life relatively difficult to go through. These days it is impossible to go through a day without hearing someone say that they are stressed. Living stressful lives has almost become a norm to many. This is why people are seeking ways to slow down, find peace, calm and clarity through all madness surrounding them. And this is where mind techniques come in to the rescue in form of self-therapy. By using mind techniques you will build up defensive walls that will help you to relieve your depression and stress so that you are more better equipped to cope with whatever problems you have.

What you think influences your mood and behaviour. The cause of depression or stress is not the events or circumstances in themselves but rather your interpretation of, and your thoughts about these events. My main reason for writing this book is to give you a better understanding of how depression and stress affect your mind and body and to show you effective ways to deal with symptoms of both conditions. Throughout this book you will learn various mind techniques and coping skills that you can practice as part of your self-help to overcome depression and stress. With this book as your guide, you have more power than anyone else to help yourself turn things around, focus on your mental well-being and getting better. Remember, what lies in your power not to do also lies in your power to do.

Contents

****

Ch. 1

Depression Generally

Emotions

Our emotions, both good and bad, are responsible for causing depression and stress in our lives. Therefore it's not possible to talk about depression and stress without exploring emotions. What are emotions anyway? Emotions are feelings or sensations brought on by other people or life events. Our thoughts and feelings have a massive impact on our emotions. There are many types of emotions which include anger, sadness, grief, worry, frustration, anxiety, guilt, shame, jealousy, resentment, hate, fear, happiness, hope, pride, anticipation, excitement, love, confidence, optimism, arousal. When we feel something we consequently respond to that feeling, the emotions in depression are predominantly negative whereas even though stress can cause some negative emotions, it can sometimes induce positive emotions too like excitement, anticipation and arousal, a good example is person who has been promoted at work, they can feel very stressed out of excitement and anticipation of what lies ahead. As regards a greater number of people who suffer from depression experience intense negative emotions that prevent them from thinking and behaving rationally and seeing the bigger picture. When this happens they only tend to see what is in front of them which leads to an even deeper downward spiral. True in life we all experience loss and other heart breaking events, which is unfortunately part of our existence. For example when you lose someone you love your emotions go into overdrive leaving you with this pain and anger that embeds your entire being and because grief doesn't happen overnight you feel as though you lose your beloved one piece by piece everyday over a long time, its emotionally draining. But the great thing about humanity is that we heal over time and yes it gets better although there's no time flame for this.

Emotions do tend to run high in most kinds of loss be it divorce, separation, loss of health, job, home and other losses that we incur in life. But however tasking it is, accept the pain you are feeling as part of your recovery and if you feel like crying do exactly that as crying can be healing in itself, when you cry you release some of the pent up emotions stored inside you. The worst thing to do is try and suppress your emotions because they will come at some point worst still aggressively or destructively. Do not see yourself as a failure either, its very easy for people to feel as though they've failed and blame themselves when they are at rock bottom. Sometimes you might need to change the way you are thinking about the situation more positively, by doing so you will begin to feel better almost immediately because your thoughts lead directly to your feelings. Its equally important to learn how to listen, identify and understand your emotions as this will put you in a better position to control them other than them controlling you. And most of all remember life is a journey of discovering and learning, the only failure you will encounter will be when you say "I give up" you are not alone either, there are millions of people right now feeling and thinking as you are but the difference will be between those who get up and make a decision to give life another shot and those who don't. Be among those who do because life always offers you a second chance which is tomorrow. And for those who are thinking "I've had enough" before you give up think of all the reasons why you've held on all this long.

There is no one 'fit' definition for depression as it is a very complex illness. It is a very common illness which can affect anyone and can vary between sufferers ranging from mild to moderate or severe. The World Health Organisation estimates that approximately 450 million people throughout the world struggle with mental health problems, with depression being one of the major problems.

Statistics show that 1 in 4 people in the United Kingdom will suffer from a mental health problem in a given year, with depression and anxiety being the most common mental illnesses. It is also shown that women are more likely than men to have received treatment for mental illness. Approximately 29% of women will suffer from a mental illness compared to 17% of men and 1 in 4 women will report depression compared to 1 in 10 in men, with suggested reasons being that men are less likely to report depression, preferring to live with it and not seek help.

What does depression feel like?

A majority of sufferers will tell you that it is very hard to deal with depression, which in turn affects both the sufferer, family, friends and work colleagues. Sufferers with mild depression will have a diminished interest in the things that they always found enjoyable, but will nevertheless try to carry on with their lives as normal. This is the most common aspect of depression and the sufferer can get by without any medication.

Moderate depression will affect most areas of the sufferer's life, for instance relationships, work and social activities and a majority of symptoms of depression will be clearly evident as a person struggles through daily life. Suicidal thoughts are very common.

Severe depression will manifest through the inability to operate at all and is characterized by intense negative feelings and also obsessive thoughts of death or suicide, isolation, weight gain or loss and trouble getting out of bed. Depression not only affects mood, it also affects behaviour and changes in thought process and physical symptoms. Behaviourally, a severely depressed person may talk more slowly than normal or appear to be restless and irritated and also isolate themselves. Changes will include extreme negative thinking, for example self blame, low self-worth, self-critic, self-hatred, self-bullying, self-labelling, inner conflict, judging themselves, inability to concentrate or make decisions. Physical effects will include changes in appetite, sleep problems, headaches, unexplained aches, pains and low energy levels.

Depression in children

Children also suffer from depression, but most of the time depression in children is overlooked and is mistaken for normal sadness and the emotions that accompany it. Any changes in a child's behaviour with no external or physical cause should not be overlooked. Depression in children is real and should not be confused with normal moodiness, it should be taken as seriously as it is for adults.

Depression is less common in children under 12 years and usually starts in the teen years. If you notice sad feelings in a child that do not go away for long periods affecting their normal activities like school work, interests, hobbies and family life then this is cause for alarm. Depression affects each individual differently so not all children will have the same symptoms, some will continue to function normally having bouts of sadness and blues every now and then, whereas others will have a dramatic change in their social activities like losing interest in everything. If you know your child well, signs that they are depressed will be easier to spot. These will be mainly changes in their normal behaviour which others wouldn't notice. Even small changes can be significant . Some children will open up about their feelings, whereas others will bottle them up especially children in their teens. Those who keep their feelings in will only show symptoms through mood swings and challenging behaviour.

As it is for adults, life events, changes and loss can bring on depression in children. Other circumstances that can underlie depression in children are; being bullied at school, feeling lonely at school, fear of failing and getting bad grades, death of a family member or beloved pet, new step family, house move, physical, emotional and sexual abuse, parents arguing frequently, witnessing, domestic violence, terminal or chronic illness in the family and feeling left out. If at any point you suspect your child to be suffering from depression, it is advisable to seek help from a doctor or mental health practitioner as soon as possible so that the child can get proper treatment. The sooner the treatment, the sooner the recovery.

Depression in women

As mentioned above, depression is more common in women than in men, with surveys consistently finding that about twice as many women as men suffer from depression. This notion is based on a number of factors, one being that women are more accepting and in touch with their feelings and opening up about them than men. As a result, they are prone to reporting feelings of depression and seeking help. Several other biological factors that may increase the risk of depression in women include;

Puberty: Hormone changes during puberty may increase a girl's risk of developing depression. After puberty, depression rates are higher in females than in males, this is due to the fact that girls go into puberty before boys and as a result more likely to develop depression at an earlier age than boys.

Premenstrual problems: Premenstrual symptoms like bloating and pain, breast tenderness, anxiety, anger, agitation, mood swings can trigger depression - premenstrual dysphoric disorder.(PMDD)

Pregnancy: Hormonal changes that take place during pregnancy can affect mood together with other pregnancy issues like relationship problems, lifestyle changes, excessive weight gain, lack of support, unwanted pregnancy, previous pregnancy complications or postpartum depression and ceasing to use anti depressant medications.

Postpartum Depression: After birth, many women find it hard to cope with the new changes that are associated with having a baby. Postpartum depression can't be mistaken for baby blues because it's signs and symptoms are more intense and last longer or do not go away until they are treated.

Menopause: The risk of depression in women may also increase during menopause, this being caused by significant reduction in oestrogen levels, causing symptoms that can eventually develop into depression, such as poor sleep, anxiety, stress, mood swings, hot flushes and weight gain among others. Early menopause or menopause caused by medical intervention for instance removal of ovaries can also trigger depression.

Workload among women can also contribute to depression. Women are well known for their multitasking skills for instance being a wife, a mother, running the household, work responsibilities, caring for elderly or sick relatives and single motherhood. all these circumstances may increase the risk of depression in a female.

Inequality in women: Oppression in relationships where women find themselves with less or no control at all. Physical, emotional and sexual abuse is very common and all of these can trigger depression.

Dietary Issues: This is another trigger of depression in women, as women are more body conscious than men and more likely to go on diets, suffer from Bulimia, Anorexia and other eating disorders.

Depression in men

Men experience depression in different ways to women and will find it hard to report or talk about their feelings. They will tend to focus on the physical symptoms of depression like headaches, back pain, low sex drive, lack of or excessive sleep. In this manner the underlying depression will go untreated but with serious repercussions. Society overall, has a narrow view of how men should handle their emotions, expecting them to be strong, macho and in control at all times which unfortunately results in many men masking their feelings to avoid being labelled 'wimps' or being seen as weak.

****

Ch. 2

Types of Depression

1-Major depression
2-Bipolar disorder
3-Post Natal Depression(PND)
4-Seasonal Affective Disorder(SAD)
5-Psychotic Depression
6-Premenstrual Dysphoric Disorder(PMDD)
7-Dysthymia depression
 8-Atypical depression

Major Depression

Also known as clinical depression or unipolar meaning one extreme of depressed mood, this is one of the most serious type of depression that affects millions of people around the world. It is characterized by long periods of low moods and negatively affects the way a person thinks and behaves thereby reducing their quality of life. For a person to be diagnosed with major depression, they have to have at least five symptoms and the symptoms must be present for most of the day and nearly everyday for at least two consecutive weeks and they must include one or both of the first two symptoms listed below;

- o A depressed mood
- o Loss of interest in all activities
- o Change in appetite
- o Sleep problems
- o Change in physical effects of depression
- o Decreased energy, tiredness and fatigue
- o Sense of worthlessness or guilt
- o Difficulties concentrating or making decisions
- o Thoughts of death or suicide

Bipolar Disorder

Also known as manic depression, this is a condition that affects moods which swing from one extreme to the other. 'Bi polar' literally means two poles or extremes. This change in mood can happen gradually over weeks or months and affects 1 in every 100 adults, it usually starts at the ages 15-19. It rarely starts after the age of 40 or earlier in childhood. Bipolar disorder is frequently inherited with genetic factors accounting for approximately 80% of the cause of the condition.

A person who suffers from bipolar will have periods of;

- o Depression- feeling low and lethargic
- o Mania- feeling very high and over active

During episodes of depression a person will have intense feelings of hopelessness which can, potentially, lead to thoughts of suicide and that is where it is very important to contact a doctor for help as soon as possible. During the manic phase of bipolar depression, the sufferer may feel incredibly high and on top of the world, making over-the-top plans, being very creative, buying things that they can't possibly afford. Most often all these plans end up in frustration because they don't work out. They may also lose their appetite, have problems getting to sleep and also experience symptoms of psychosis (seeing and hearing things that are not there). Living with bipolar disorder can be very challenging due to the high and low phases of the disorder which are often so extreme that they interfere with everyday life. The good news is that bipolar disorder is treatable with medication, psychological treatment- talking therapies and lifestyle adaptation such as regular exercise, eating the right diet, and plenty of sleep and rest.

Bipolar is a chronic and relapsing illness that requires long-term medical treatment combined with therapy, lifestyle changes and social support.

Types of Bipolar disorder

Bipolar 1 disorder- involves at least one manic episode and one or more major depression episodes.

Bipolar 2 disorder- is defined by a pattern of depressive episodes and hypomanic episodes.

Cyclothymic disorder- experiencing both hypomania and depressive mood swings over a course of 2 years. The symptoms of this type of bipolar disorder are not severe enough to meet the criteria to be diagnosed from bipolar type 1 or bipolar type 2.

Post Natal Depression

PND is a type of depression some women experience after having a baby. It can appear within the first six weeks of giving birth. Research suggests that PND is a result of tiredness ' lack of sleep and the major changes that having a new baby brings about. PND is so common that it is considered normal, affecting 1 in 10 women and can sometimes go unnoticed. New fathers can also be affected by it. This type of depression can range from being mild to very severe. PND is very different from baby blues and is unlikely to go away very quickly without help. If it is recognised, it is advisable to seek help very quickly before it becomes a long-term problem.

Seasonal Affective Disorder

SAD is a type of depression that has a seasonal pattern whereby episodes of depression tend to occur at the same time each year. The symptoms begin at the end of autumn when the days are getting shorter with severe episodes in December, January and February. SAD starts with symptoms of low mood and loss of interest in daily life and also reduced activity and socialising. Lack of sunlight in the winter is believed to be the cause of SAD as sunlight triggers the production of serotonin in the brain. Serotonin is a hormone in the brain that is responsible for keeping moods stable and positive. SAD usually improves in the spring, eventually disappearing.

Psychotic Depression

This is a very serious mental illness which requires hospitalisation. It is a subtype of major depression that occurs when a severe depressive illness includes some form of psychosis which manifests as hallucinations and delusions, because of this the sufferer thinks and believes that they can hear and see things that clearly don't exist. People suffering from this illness will struggle to get through the day and may stay sleep all day and then stay awake all night, neglecting hygiene.

Pre Menstrual Dysphoric Disorder

This is a condition where by a woman has severe depression symptoms before her menstrual flow or cycle. This occurs about 5-11 days before a woman starts her monthly cycle and it affects 2% to 10% of menstruating women.

The symptoms of PMMD are similar to those of premenstrual syndrome but more severe. Living with PMDD is extremely painful and if left untreated can be disruptive to the sufferer and everyone around her.

Dysthymia depression

Dysthymia depression is a chronic mild form of depression which has fewer symptoms than major depression. It usually lasts for at least 2 years or longer and people who suffer from dysthymia generally experience intense periods of dark moods and are very critical of themselves and tend to worry a lot, feel guilty and suffer from very low self-worth, hence losing their ability to enjoy life and function normally. This type of depression affects more women than men.

Atypical depression

Atypical means 'abnormal'. This type of depression has symptoms that are not usually found in people suffering from other forms of depression. A person with atypical depression will respond to good news and when positive events take place. Their moods strongly react to what's going on around them, good or bad. Atypical depression occurs as a feature of major depression or dysthymic depression.

****

Ch.3

Causes of Depression

Whilst it is not clearly known what causes depression, there are a number of factors that contribute to its development. People develop depression for numerous reasons, but the following are among the most common ones.

o   Stressful events: A number of stressful events can trigger depression such as loss of a loved one, divorce, relationship breakdown, financial difficulties, loss of income/job, homelessness, retirement, child custody court cases, giving birth and many more.

o   Genetics: A family history of depression may increase the risk. If several members in the family have suffered from depression in the past then it is likely that someone will become depressed themselves.

o   Personal circumstances: For example isolation and loneliness will make a person more likely to get depressed as they will have no one to share their problems, worries and concerns with, having to deal with these on their own.

o   Serious illness: Some serious illnesses put a person at risk of developing depression especially potentially life threatening ones like cancer, HIV and heart disease as they affect people mentally, physically and emotionally. Also long term chronic illnesses, for instance arthritis, asthma, Alzheimer's, cystic fibrosis, diabetes, heart disease, eating disorders, obesity, osteoporosis and back pain, may make life unbearable which may eventually lead to depression. Other reoccurring conditions and infections can all contribute to depression. Head injuries are also often known to cause depression as they trigger mood swings and emotional problems.

o Medication: Some medications appear to cause depression by altering brain chemicals in some way. These drugs cause certain feelings like sadness, mood swings, and despair which are all associated with depression.

o Alcohol and drug abuse: People who take drugs for instance Heroin, Cocaine, and Marijuana are at a high risk of developing an addiction. Addicts experience their highs and lows when they use drugs and it is during their lows when the drugs have worn off that they are more vulnerable to depression. Alcohol dependence on the other hand can also trigger depression and other serious health conditions.

o Abuse: Past childhood traumatic physical, emotional and sexual abuse can cause depression later in life.

Major depression triggers

o Job loss
o Death of a loved one
o Illness
o Abuse- physical, emotional and sexual
o Family history
o Medication
o Drugs and alcohol
o Childbirth

Bipolar disorder triggers

Stressful positive or negative life events will trigger the symptoms of bipolar disorder, for example marriage, having a baby, job promotion, new job, new relationship, relationship breakdown, house move, income or job loss, divorce, death of a family member and physical or chronic illness. Other triggers include:

o Childhood trauma- it is believed that suffering from stressful situations in childhood may trigger bipolar depression such as abuse, neglect, loss and grief.
o Alcohol abuse, drug abuse
o Sleeping pattern disruptions
o Stressful work situations

Post Natal Depression triggers

o Depression during pregnancy
o A traumatic birth

o   Relationship problems
o   Lack of support from family, friends
o   Having no close family members around for support
o   Physical health problems before and after birth
o   Health complications with the new born baby

Seasonal Affective Disorder triggers

o   Lack of sunlight
o   Low serotonin levels especially in the winter months
o   High melatonin levels- the hormone which makes us sleep- although its still not clear, it is known that people who suffer from SAD produce more of this hormone in the winter than other people.
o   Stressful events like a new diet after Christmas into the new year as a result of gaining weight over the Christmas period, money worries related to Christmas expenses, bereavement, physical illness, use of drugs and alcohol.

Psychotic depression triggers

o   Genes – this illness can run in families although other people who have no family members that suffer from it can also develop psychotic illness.
o   Stressful life events can trigger psychotic depression
o   Certain medications for example steroids can also contribute to triggering this condition

Pre Menstrual Dysphoric Disorder triggers

o   Hormonal changes related to the menstrual cycle

- o Chemical changes in the brain
- o Lifestyle factors like not eating the right diet, not exercising, weight gain
- o Stress

Dysthymia depression triggers

- o Imbalances in the brain
- o Family history of dysthymia
- o Traumatic events
- o Stress
- o Gender- women suffer from it more than men
- o Chronic physical illness
- o Other mental disorders

Atypical depression triggers

- o Traumatic events
- o Serious illness
- o Negative feelings and thoughts about self and conflicts
- o Abuse- physical, emotional or sexual
- o Family history of depression
- o Drugs or alcohol abuse

****

Ch.4

Symptoms of Depression

The symptoms of depression can be complex and difficult to recognize and if left untreated the symptoms may get worse and last for a long period of time. The symptoms of depression will often manifest as physical, psychological and social and will vary widely between people.

Psychological symptoms include;

o Continuous low mood or sadness
o Feeling restless, irritability and agitation
o Becoming tearful easily
o Feeling hopeless, numb, despairing, worthless
o Difficulty concentrating
o Inability to make decisions
o Negative irrational thinking
o Low energy and fatigue
o Anxiety and worry
o Suicidal thoughts or attempts
o Lack of motivation or interest to do things
o Not finding any enjoyment out of life

Physical symptoms

o An increased or decreased appetite
o Disturbed sleep either sleeping more, less or none at all
o Unexplained aches and pains
o Feeling tired or low energy levels
o Headaches
o Dizziness and feeling light or fainting
o Moving or speaking more slowly than usual
o Loss of interest in sex- low libido
o Use of drugs, alcohol, tobacco

Social symptoms

o Not taking part in the activities that you used to enjoy
o Difficulty socialising
o Avoiding social events
o Cutting off contact from family and friends, living in isolation or as a recluse
o Not doing well at work or studies

+

Bipolar Disorder symptoms during the depression phase

o Feeling sad and hopeless
o Low energy levels
o Suicidal thoughts
o Difficulty concentrating and remembering things
o Loss of appetite
o Difficulty sleeping
o Feelings of guilt, despair, emptiness, confusion
o Self-doubt and low self-confidence

- Loss of interest in daily activities
- Being delusional
- Having hallucinations
- Illogical thinking
- Being negative about everything

Bipolar Disorder symptoms during the manic phase

- Talking very quickly
- High energy levels
- Full of positivity
- Feeling very happy
- Being creative- with a lot of ideas and exciting plans
- Easily irritated
- Eating less or not eating at all
- Feelings of self-importance
- Lack of sleep
- Making irrational and abrupt risky decisions
- Being delusional
- Having hallucinations
- Illogical thinking

Symptoms of Post Natal Depression

- Continuous low mood and sadness
- Lack of energy and feeling tired most of the time
- Lack of interest in the baby
- Loss of interest in activities and life in general
- Disturbed sleep
- Low self-esteem and confidence

o Feeling guilty
o Suicidal thoughts and self harm
o Increase or decrease in weight as a result of increase or decrease in appetite
o Tearful for no apparent reason
o Unable to cope or look after the new baby
o Hostility towards partner
o Loss of libido

Symptoms of Seasonal Affective Disorder

o Feeling sad and low
o Agitation, despair, irritable, worthless, tearful
o Feeling tired and sleeping a lot
o Reduced sex drive
o Feeling anxious and stressed
o Indecisiveness
o Increase in appetite
o Reduced or less active than normal

Symptoms of Psychotic Disorder

o Agitation
o Anxiety
o Sleeping less or excessively
o Delusions and hallucinations
o Suicide thoughts
o Eating more or less
o Irritable and angry
o Loss of focus and concentration

o Lack of interest in everyday activities
o Low energy

Symptoms of Pre Menstrual Dysphoric Disorder

o Feeling bloated
o Pain and discomfort in the abdomen
o Breast pain
o Headaches
o Weight gain
o Insomnia
o Muscle and joint pain
o Backache
o Mood swings, irritability and anger
o Extremely low moods, sadness – being emotional and tearful
o Restlessness, clumsiness and tiredness
o Confusion and forgetfulness
o Low self-esteem
o Loss of libido
o Change in appetite
o Decreased interest in daily activities

Symptoms of dysthymia depression

o Feelings of sadness
o Changes in appetite
o Low energy levels
o Changes in sleep pattern- sleeping too much or too little
o Difficulty concentrating or indecisiveness

- o Feeling hopeless, low self-esteem, self-critical, negative thinking
- o Lack of interest in normal activities

Atypical depression symptoms

- o Sleeping too much
- o Increased appetite
- o Sensitivity to rejection or criticism
- o Fatigue

****

Ch.5

Coping with Depression

Owing to the fact that depression affects people in different ways and is triggered by varying factors in each individual, equally, there is a whole range of methods, approaches and treatments for treating it. One approach or treatment may work for one person but not for the other person. People with depression find it hard to function normally and therefore this makes it even harder for them to make a choice and get the help that they need, as they are often enveloped in this dark cloud of self doubt and negative thinking and thinking that its probably best to give up than trying at all. You have more power over depression than you think.

To start with, if you think and feel that you are depressed and you recognise all the symptoms mentioned in the chapter before, your first stop should be your doctor however much you find it difficult, drag yourself because if you don't do anything the problem is going to grow and get worse, a stitch in time saves nine, don't be embarrassed either to talk to your doctor, I can't emphasise enough that depression is an illness, doctors are human beings too and see people everyday who are depressed. If it's the idea of having to take depression medications that's putting you off, you don't have to because there are other alternative therapies that your doctor can refer you to that could work out amazingly for you. Also important in your recovery is your support network of family and friends.

These will play an important role in helping you to recover and stay well. If you are close enough to them then open up to them about your condition. The sooner you unburden yourself the better for you, you will feel uplifted, lighter and it will also make you realise that people actually do care about you and your well-being. And if you are unfortunate to be in a situation where you are not close enough to your family or they live abroad or you do not have any close friends that you can confide in, there is a solution for you too, charities like the Samaritans and Mind are there for people like you who need a listening ear, they offer advice and support to any one suffering from emotional distress as well as being supportive and caring.

For those people who are suffering from mild to moderate depression, this book will give you access to mind techniques that will open your mind to new ideas or thought processes and also find more effective ways to cope with your depression. Because depression brings about so many changes in the person suffering from it from the way they think, feel and behave which is always negative, the depressed person will always think worse out of every situation, activities will be abandoned, they have low self-esteem, self doubt, feel guilty about a lot of things neither will they eat or sleep properly. Therefore a change in thinking and behaviour will be crucial in coping with depression. For when your thoughts begin to change from negative to positive, you will feel far much better. Healthy positive thinking helps prevent and control depression, whereas thinking negatively will worsen it because behaviours are a product of thoughts. True it will take time for you to be able to change your thought patterns and recondition them again to positive but with daily practice and patience you will see changes.

Depression and a healthy diet

While depression needs to be dealt with by a trained professional, there are many things that you can do to help promote your mental health and a healthy balanced diet is one of them. Nutrition plays a big role in mental health, there is a vast amount of evidence that shows that diet and mental health have a link. So to say, a healthy diet plays a big role in developing , managing and keeping at bay mental health problems. Therefore the right diet is vital to mental health as it is to physical health.

Eating well promotes health and prevents many illnesses. Eating three balanced meals a day which are breakfast, lunch and dinner will do tremendous good when you're suffering from depression. Drugs, alcohol, caffeine, and sugary foods should be avoided as they will make you anxious and complicate your depression symptoms and also disrupt your sleeping pattern. As well as eating a balanced diet everyday, the following foods have also been known to boost moods;

o   Omega3- these healthy fatty acids contribute towards healthy balanced levels of serotonin the hormone in our brain responsible for mood lifting examples of these are fish- sardines, trout, tuna

o   Plenty of fruit and vegetables

o Vitamin B- this vitamin affects brain function, mental focus and mood. Vitamin B12 is essential for normal brain and nervous system function found in egg yolk, salmon, liver

o Vitamin D- The sunshine vitamin- when exposed to the sun our bodies consume it. Lack of sunlight is linked to SAD.

o Selenium- research suggests that selenium decreases depression. It is found in nuts especially brazil nuts, whole grains, beans, sea food and lean meats.

Given that over-eating or under-eating are some of the signs of depression, if you are over-weight or obese, it is advisable that you try and lose weight as you are also at risk of health problems like diabetes, heart problems, stroke and others, avoid going on diets, not only will they not work but they will also leave you worse off gaining more weight than before, this is to say that if you are aiming to lose weight do it steadily and responsibly for permanent results. Eat three balanced meals everyday of proteins, fats and carbohydrates, vitamins and minerals with lots of fruit and vegetables, do not be tempted to skip meals because this will cause you to snack on high calorie foods, cut back on fat, sugar and salt. If you chose to snack go for healthy choices snacks like un-salted nuts, seed, fruits, vegetable sticks and other healthy snacks.

On the other hand if you are eating less being under-weight can damage your health and contribute to a weakened immune system, fragile bones and feeling tired. If you are under-weight, check with your doctor for help and advice, also eat a healthy balanced diet with the right amount of calories for your height and activity levels.

Depression and Exercise

Exercise has numerous health benefits to mental health as it has for physical health and can aid in the recovery from depression as well as preventing it happening in the first place. Exercise can benefit anyone who is depressed from mild to severe depression. If you are concerned about the effects of exercise on your overall health ask your doctor about exercise on prescription programme. After you have chosen the right exercise for you, make it a point that it is something you enjoy, this will help your continuity. Even if you can manage very little exercise it will still benefit you, frankly speaking any activity however little is better than none! When you engage in exercise endorphins are released, these are the body's natural pain killers, they boost your moods positively, reduce your stress levels, boosts your self-esteem, increase your energy levels, and improve your sleep. Exercise doesn't have to be very energetic to ease depression, do it at the pace you can manage and make sure you stick to your routine or exercise plan, however low you feel some days you have to keep going, these are days when you need the exercise more to lift your moods, keeping active will also act as a distraction from your depression symptoms. People who exercise daily have reported feeling that when they exercise they feel uplifted, positive, more confident and think clearly. So don't miss out on these benefits.

The ideal amount of exercise should be 30 minutes to an hour a day for most days of the week to be able to cultivate more health benefits but like said before little exercise is better than none. This can be walking, swimming, running, cycling, skipping, dancing, or house work like gardening, cleaning, washing the car or DIY.

Depression and sleep

Suffering from depression can bring about disruptions in sleeping patterns for instance not sleeping at all or very little or sleeping too much. Difficulty getting to sleep is a major symptom for most people suffering from depression. Causing;

- o Difficulty falling asleep
- o Over-sleeping
- o Difficulty staying asleep
- o Difficulty waking up early in the morning
- o Sleeping during the day
- o Poor quality of sleep
- o Waking up exhausted

Insomnia is not only inclined to contribute to depression, but also to other mental illnesses like anxiety disorders, psychotic disorders as well as physical disorders such as infections, high blood pressure, obesity and diabetes.

These are some of the easy tips that you can apply to relive insomnia;

- o Treat your bedroom as your sanctuary for sleeping, don't take work into your bedroom, make sure it's quiet and dark.

o Eat a healthy balanced diet of three meals a day. Don't over-eat or under-eat as this will disturb your sleep.

o Have your regular exercise during the day but not prior to sleeping . Regular exercise will boost your sleep and increase its quality.

o Have a sleep routine with regular sleeping times and aim for sleeping at least 7-8 hours of sleep a night.

o Avoid use of drugs, alcohol, caffeine and tobacco.

o Avoid napping during the day as this will prevent you from sleeping at night.

o Use relaxation techniques, deep breathing, meditation or prayer before you go to bed, these relaxation techniques will calm your body and mind and also promote your sleep.

o Listening to relaxing music, reading a book, watching a relaxing television programme can all prepare you for a relaxing sleep.

o Sleep on a comfortable bed and pillow and make sure they are supportive enough.

****

Ch. 6

Mind Techniques for Depression Relief

_____

Hypnosis:

Hypnosis is a trance like natural state of focused attention and concentration. When you are under hypnosis you get into a calm relaxed state, in this state your subconscious mind is more open to any suggestions given in forms of new ways of thinking, habits, beliefs, and behaviours,. It is the power and intelligence of the subconscious mind that makes all these changes possible. This is to say that hypnosis is a tool used to gain access to the subconscious mind, when you are in hypnosis your conscious mind goes to rest whereas your subconscious mind comes forward or is revealed. It is in the subconscious mind that all the data from the past in particular, beliefs, fears, attitudes, thoughts have been stored and it is through the subconscious mind that this data can be accessed to help you gain control over your negative thoughts, behaviours, habits, beliefs by re-programming the subconscious mind.

Hypnosis is often performed by a hypnotherapist using verbal repetition and mental imaginations by use of suggestions. Hypnosis can also be a self-therapy hence self-hypnosis. However in sufferers with a history of depression, they will respond positively to hypnosis only when it is used as a tool to more in-depth psychotherapy, this also applies to people who are suffering from psychosis and some personality disorders. Although hypnosis can be used to treat depression, its strongly advised that in cases of severe depression, consult your psychiatrist or physician who will accurately diagnose your symptoms and mark out the boundaries of your depression.

Hypnosis for depression

Hypnosis is now widely recognised as a health care tool. Hypnosis provides an effective way to access a depressed person's subconscious mind where the negative self-defeating and sabotaging thoughts and behaviours are embedded. Here new hypnotic suggestions will be implanted to help correct their thinking pattern, their behaviours, restless sleep patterns, unhealthy eating patterns and habits, low self-esteem, increase motivation and eliminating or reducing negative thinking which is a major contributor to depression.

Hypnosis for depression will positively;

o Improve your appetite

o Help you feel calm, clear minded and relaxed

o Feel more confident and boost self-esteem

o You will be more focussed, motivated, and able to concentrate more.

o You will have more interest in activities and enjoying your social life again and the company of others.

o You will be in a better position to handle past negative experiences, accept them and deal with the emotions that come with them.

o Hypnosis will bring about improvement in quality of sleep, enabling you to enjoy your sleep and wake up feeling refreshed.

Some recent studies have shown that hypnosis is more effective than CBT which is the most common therapy used in treating clinical depression. Hypnosis doesn't work for everyone but if you're one of those people who are struggling with depression and have not found any relief from medication or psychotherapy then hypnotherapy is worth a try. Hypnosis is natural and safe, many people with mental health issues have benefited from it and are continuing to use it as it gains momentum. For sufferers of mild or moderate depression this simple self-hypnosis script will help you with your negative thinking process, incorporate new responses into your life, to become positively happier, calmer and feel more clearer in your mind. You will have to be repetitive with your self-hypnosis until you feel better.

How to use your script

o You can get someone who you know to read you the script but they have to be committed to doing this everyday without fail. If this is not an option then record your script. When you're recording your script make sure that you use the right tone of voice and you can add anything that you want to add to your script as long as its positive.

o Put aside time everyday to listen to your self-hypnosis script.

o Practice in a quiet and comfortable place which is relaxing for you.

o Practice everyday.

Self-Hypnosis script for depression relief

I will make myself as comfortable as I can .... I will take a nice deep breath in .....close my eyes ...... and begin to relax ...... just thinking about relaxing every muscle in my body ...... from the top of my head to the tips of my toes ...... as I begin to focus attention on my breathing ...... my awareness of everything around me will decrease .....

I let all the muscles in my face relax ..... starting with muscles around my eyes and as I concentrate on relaxing this area every muscle in my body will relax ..... I will then let the muscles around my jaws and mouth relax .... feeling limp and loose as my lips part slightly letting go of all the tension .... this relaxation spreads to my shoulders and neck .... then to my arms and back ...... relaxing all those muscles completely .... now I notice the same feeling moving into my abdomen ...... to my thighs and legs .... past my knees, ankles feet and into my toes ...... soothing, calming and relaxing all my body .... as I continue to breath in and out slowly .... I relax even more and more drifting into a deeper and deeper level of relaxation ...... I am feeling lighter and lighter ..... floating higher and higher into a deeper level of relaxation ..... I am now completely relaxed .... more relaxed than I have ever felt before ......as I experience this beautiful feeling of peace and calm .... I let go of my mind .... drifting ...... relaxing .... and drifting ......

Now I am imagining myself in my special place .... this is a very special place for me .... I can feel it and see it in my mind .... feeling my body relax .... deeper and deeper...... enjoying these positive feelings .... I am feeling lighter and lighter..........floating higher and higher into a comfortable relaxation ....

Because I am now relaxed I let any feelings I have buried come up to the surface ..... I now allow the emotions that are arising within me pass right through me ....sadness, anger, disappointment, negativity, guilt, frustration, agitation, anxiety ...... I am letting all my emotions surface and float to the top. Feelings of fear .... feelings of loss .... feelings of resentment .... I let them all float and surface to the top ...... there is no need for me to resist I let my body relax and as I drift into a deeper relaxation ...... I let myself forgive all the things I have blamed ..... I forgive each person ...... I forgive myself .... I feel a compassion enter my heart ..... I let go of all the anger, sadness and pain I have been feeling ..... I let it pass ......

I am feeling it pass through me and out of me .... and as I let these emotions go I feel a new sense of peace emerge ...... with each day that passes by I feel happier in mind and body ...... I feel more content in myself and this wonderful suggestion that I'm feeling more happier and content will grow stronger in my mind with each day I know I can make it and I know I can do it ...... I know I have the courage to move ahead beyond my depression ..... that my body and spirit will heal..... each day I grow stronger ..... healing and recovering ...... getting better and better with each day that goes by .... I am drifting and floating in a warm glow of healing energy ...... there is no need to resist .... drifting ...... floating and relaxing. Depression is a healing process it's okay for me to allow myself to grieve and be sad .... and when I have completed the time of sadness .... I will set myself free ..... the time will soon be over for those feelings ..... and I will feel free from them ..... I will feel free .... because I can accept and get rid of any feelings ...... discard any feelings I am through with ...... I can let them come and go ......

come and go as I go through them ...... now I will continue to relax .... feeling myself relax with my feelings .... and think of how I am a whole person with many feelings that make me whole and healthy ......

I go through my day feeling fine ...... I watch the anxiety and sadness drift away from me ...... leaving me feeling calm and relaxed .... every time I hear the word relax my body and mind will relax even more and more ...... every muscle in my body will relax ..... my mind will become even more calmer ...... I am a calm person and act in ways that make me feel good ..... and as I relax more with each breath .... My subconscious mind will accept these suggestions and I will start to notice with each day I become more happier and positive in my thinking, feelings and behaviour .... and these new ways will grow stronger and stronger in my mind and they will be part of me ...... and because I now have new responses to old situations ..... when I think about things that bring me sadness, anxiety, worry and depression ......I will not feel anxious, sad, guilty, resentful, angry or disappointed ...... I will rather breath deeply in and out and relax feeling love, happiness, compassion, forgiveness, hope and peace .... feeling calm and relaxed .... my new response will make me feel strong, calm and free ...... my days will be full of Accomplishments and I will be pleased with my accomplishments .... I will feel good about myself because I have new responses that are making my day more pleasant...... I am calm, strong and free from depression .... I'm more clearer in my mind and able to cope with any challenges ...... with a tremendous confidence and self- control because I'm in charge now of how I think, feel and behave ......feeling calm and relaxed ......

I will continue to enjoy my special place for another moment .... experience it ....and relax .... until I am ready to come back to full awareness ...... and when I am ready to come back I will count from one to five ...... and as count to five I will open my eyes and come back feeling relaxed and at peace ....

1.................... Beginning to come back
2.................... Coming up
3.................... Feeling relaxed
4.................... Beginning to open your eyes
5.................... I open my eyes and come back all the way feeling wonderful

Neuro Linguistic Programming (NLP) for depression
NLP is a method of influencing brain behaviour through the use of language to enable a person to re-arrange the way their brain

responds to the programming to bring about new and better behaviours. In short, NLP explorers habits, thought patterns and how these play a role in the way we behave and act.

The principles of NLP are that;

o There is always possibility of change.
o You are in charge of your mind and therefore in control of bringing about the desired changes you want.
o You are not your behaviour, you are always free to change a behaviour.
o You posses all the resources you need to achieve success and all your desired goals.
o There is no failure, only feedback. The reasoning behind this is to stop self-blame or blaming others for things that did or didn't happen.
o When you communicate better, you get better communication back to you.

In depression, NLP aims at helping to eliminate negative thoughts and to develop behaviour that will help you to realise your full potential and also to feel better with positive coping strategies.

The NLP practitioner will re-wire or re-programme your thinking pattern to induce positivity and lift moods by use of NLP techniques outlined below;

Reframing- changing how you see a situation or putting a different spin on it. For instance if you missed an important appointment but then you managed to go and catch up with family or friends or went back home to do errands which needed doing which is a positive!

The use of metaphor - this is communicating with the subconscious mind by use of stories, poems, jokes, analogies to access the subconscious mind so that underlying issues can be resolved.

NLP is a very powerful technique based on the power of the mind, by using these techniques with the help of a NLP practitioner, you can learn to take control of your mind and how to respond to the events that happen in your life. Whilst you can't control these events you can control how you react to them.

Relaxation and breathing techniques for depression relief

Relaxation is a state of being completely calm and at rest physically and mentally. Being relaxed and free from tension has many healthy benefits for both body and mind. Relaxing is a way of life and therefore should be easy, when you relax your muscles become less tense, your organs slow down, blood flow in your brain increases, heart beat and breathing rates slow down.

Benefits of relaxation on the mind

o Relieves depression
o Relieves stress
o Reduces anxiety
o It lifts moods and induces positivity
o Brings about calmness and stillness

o Boosts confidence and inner strength
o Boosts memory
o Boosts creativity

Relaxation in depression

Relaxation techniques like progressive muscle relaxation (PMR) can help relieve from mild to moderate depression. The PMR technique is designed to induce both physical and mental relaxation, it works by relaxing major muscles in the body one at a time from head to toes.

Deep breathing in depression

Deep breathing has become increasingly important in relief for depression symptoms as it transforms energy from tension to relaxation. It is common to experience shallow breathing when you're depressed, which restricts the brain from receiving enough oxygen. By deep breathing you don't tense your body plus it allows the lungs to expand to their normal full capacity. Deep breathing can also help in depression by restoring balance to the brain functioning, and by doing so, more feel good hormones are released.

Benefits of deep breathing

o It relieves tension and induces relaxation for the body and mind
o It relieves emotional worries
o It improves the nervous system
o Boosts mental focus and concentration

o   Relieves stress

o   It strengthens the immune system

Positive thinking and affirmations

People affected by depression tend to think very negatively about themselves, everything around them and the future because they are in this dark place and are unable to see any light at the end of the tunnel. Depression sufferers think differently from people who don't suffer from depression as they're always in constant battle with their negative thinking and need to learn to think more positively again. Negative thinking and feelings are linked together and a combination of these two accompanied by self-blame, self-criticism, self-attack, self-hatred, self-labelling and self-harm can push you deeper into depression. When you adopt positive thinking, you are transformed by the renewing of your mind. Thinking of yourself negatively will have a bad impact on the way you view yourself which is often as a failure, a let down or worthless. You will also have a negative perspective of the world, as you will think that everyone sees you as you view yourself or you will feel that they are judging you thence you will see the future as dreary and frightening which makes you become even more depressed and so the cycle carries on in that manner unless its broken down. If this cycle is not broken, you will stay in this dark place for a very long time when you don't have to.

If you change the way you think from negative to positive, you will start to have a different view of yourself from worthless to worthy and deserving , you will start to feel that the world views you as you view yourself and you will be more hopeful and trusting of the future looking to the bright side of things and expecting good things to happen for you. It doesn't matter how long this process will take, it will take time but things will change for you and life will be worth living again.

Illness arising from depression can be exceedingly rational and bossy and is very likely to want to be the master of you and tell you how you should feel, what you can think and what you can do, unless you break its chains and free yourself. To challenge depression you will have to start with changing the way you think. If depression says 'you are weak and worthless' your immediate reply should be 'I'm strong and worthy' whatever negative thought depression chucks out at you answer back positively, by doing this you encourage your mind to take back control.

Positive affirmations for depression

Positive affirmations are words that we can affirm over and over to manifest a positive change. Positive affirmations are very helpful in depression by undoing the damage caused by the constant negative thinking and can therefore be used as an additional form of treatment in depressed people. Affirmations should be used everyday repeatedly, anywhere at any time and can be very effective with persistence.

Depression affirmations

o   I am in control of my thoughts
o   I love myself unconditionally
o   I am loved and accepted as I am

o Depression doesn't define who I am
o I am a strong human being and resilient
o I am worthy of love
o I stay positive no matter what
o I think positive thoughts that lift me up
o I am free of negative thoughts
o Being healthy is a priority to me
o I exercise regularly to clear my mind
o I eat the right foods that boost my mental health
o I am overcoming depression no matter what
o I am determined to beat depression
o I live in the present moment and appreciate life
o I am happy the way I am
o Being free from depression is a relief
o I only focus on the things that matter in life
o My mind is full of positivity
o I release all negativity in my life

****

Ch. 7

Mindfulness and Depression

Depression is the most common mental illness, up to 8% of the people who experience a major depressive episode may relapse, drugs sometimes or often lose their effectiveness if they work at all, this is when mindfulness therapy and other therapies are very important in the treating of depression.

What is mindfulness?

Mindfulness is the paying attention to the present moment and being fully aware and more observant without judging or worrying and thinking too much about the past and future. Being mindful is simply being, it brings your mind from the past and future into the now. Mindfulness originates in the ancient meditation practices. It has been connected to Buddhism but it is not a religion just a way of being or prayer, when you pray you quieten your mind and clear it of all thoughts and concentrate on your prayer, so is being mindful, being mindful brings about calm and deep relaxation of body and mind. Mindful practices include meditation, yoga and Tai-Chi.

Meditation:

Meditation is the practice of training the mind to reach a deep relaxed level of consciousness. Meditation aims at focussing and concentrating on the now eliminating any thoughts that come into the mind to steer it back to stillness. Meditation is a way to get to know the mind, its a very simple practice and can be used by anyone. A lot of people find it difficult to meditate at first, to silence the mind, patience is required here, if your mind wanders off while you are meditating, stay calm and breath in and out and gently bring your mind back to the present again and again, don't give up, with resilience and plenty of practice meditation will become easier and you will see the results soon. You can start with a few minutes everyday and increase the time length as you go by. If done regularly meditation can be a great mind exercise for depression relief.

The benefits of meditation are;

o It fights depression symptoms by improving mood and behaviour.
o Reduces anxiety
o Relieves stress
o Increases serotonin production
o Improves the immune system
o Improves quality of sleep
o Creativity increases
o Induces happiness
o Sharpens the mind, concentration and focus
o Emotional stability improves

Mindful meditation

Quieten your mind and concentrate on your breathing, and after your breathing is settled put all your focus on whatever you are doing using all your senses for instance listening to all the sounds around you, smell the air, take a look at your surroundings, the different vibrant colours you can see, if you are touching anything feel the sensations.

Take everything in and what you are feeling.

o If your mind starts to wander off or distract you in any way or form, notice these thoughts and release them then pull your mind back to concentration and awareness.
o You can practice mindful meditation for as long as you want.

Mindful yoga

The word yoga means 'to join' and originates from India. Yoga relates to the union between body, mind and spirit that yoga can bring about. Yoga focuses on strength, flexibility and breathing to boost both physical and mental well-being. The main components of yoga are posture and breathing. People suffering from depression can benefit from yoga therapy because of its gentle, calming and relaxing nature. Yoga is easily accessible as it is increasingly becoming popular in hospitals, schools, therapy centres, surgeries, clubs, fitness centres and health clubs. It is advisable to check with your doctor if you are on permanent medication or undergoing a course of treatment.

The benefits of yoga are;

o Yoga can improve symptoms of depression and the immune function
o Reduces stress

o   Eliminates anxiety

o   Induces positivity and boosts moods

o   Increases confidence and self-esteem

o   Improves sleep

o   It's relaxing and calming

Yoga practice

o   Put aside time everyday for yoga- blend it in your daily routine so that it is part of your routine, bearing in mind that yoga is one of those practices where you have to be disciplined.

o   Chose a quiet place

o   Start off slowly and listen to your body- don't push yourself too hard or over do it, take it easy and enjoy it, if you find it hard on your own joining a yoga group would be a great idea.

o   Practice on a light stomach

o   Wear comfortable clothing

o   Include a variety of yoga techniques and postures. You can look up online for ideas.

o   Be consistent- however difficult you find it at first, if you stick to it with each practice you will improve.

Mindful Tai-Chi

Tai-Chi is an old martial art practice that originated from China. It involves a series of slow meditative body movements that were originally designed for self defence and to promote inner peace and calm. Tai-Chi calms the mind and body and also improves physical strength.

Mind benefits of Tai-Chi;

o It reduces depression symptoms
o It relieves stress
o Reduces anxiety
o Improves sleep
o Improves memory

Mindfulness in depression relief

Everything happens now, this is the only moment in time. The past is just memories and thoughts whereas the future is just images and visions. If you don't live in the present moment you miss it because it won't come back.

Living in the past will cause you frustration, anger, guilt, what-ifs and depression. On the other hand, not only living in the future will rob you of enjoying the present moment, it will also make you anxious, worried and stressed.

The experience of living in the now is more enjoyable and easier than living in the past or future. Being more aware of the present moment can help you to get in touch with your body, thoughts, feelings and emotions as well as being more appreciative of life. When you are aware of your feelings and thoughts, you are heightened to experience everything afresh and it is easy for you to track down the thoughts that bring conflict within you, work through them and let them go. Paying full attention to the present in depression is essential and helpful as it can improve the symptoms of depression, for instance negative thinking, clouded thoughts, difficulty concentrating, self doubt, indecisiveness and forgetfulness. As we know, all these symptoms can be very disruptive to daily life such as work, relationships, handling of finances, social life.

Negative thinking can give way to negative emotions, self harm and suicide. Concentrating on the now helps depression sufferers to become more aware and alert to their negative thoughts acknowledging them and acting upon them before negative emotions and behaviour follow suit. There is growing evidence showing that mindfulness has proved to be very effective in preventing relapse in depressive individuals.

****

Ch.8

Getting Help for Severe Depression

Treatment for depression usually involves a combination of medicines, talking therapies, alternative therapies and self-help. To diagnose depression, a doctor, psychiatrist or a mental health practitioner will talk to the patient and hear about the specific symptoms of depression the patient has. Talking to the patient enables the doctor or specialist to learn about other things that are relevant to making a depression diagnosis. A physical examination of the patients' overall health will be carried out and a personal interview and lab tests are also carried out to rule out other conditions that may be causing the depression.

The doctor will also discuss any family history of depression or other mental illnesses and also evaluate your symptoms including when they started, how long you've had them, any medication you're taking, how you feel, your lifestyle, diet, exercise, drug or alcohol abuse and whether you have any symptoms of depression as outlined in chapter 2. It is important that you do not self-diagnose, this depression questionnaire overleaf can be used as a guide to help you assess whether you have the symptoms of depression.

See overleaf.

1. Have you found little interest in doing things? YES/NO

....

2. Have you found yourself feeling depressed?   YES/NO

....

3. Have you had trouble falling, staying asleep or sleeping too much?   YES/NO

....

4. Have you been feeling tired or with low energy? YES/NO

....

5. Have you been eating too much or very little? YES/NO

....

6. Have you felt guilty or worthless? YES/NO

....

7. Have you felt that you're a failure or let other people down? YES/NO

....

8. Have you had trouble concentrating on things? YES/NO

....

9. Have you had difficulty making decisions? YES/NO

....

10 .Have you felt agitated? YES/NO

....

11. Have you slowed down in movement or speaking? YES/NO

....

12 .Have you had suicide thoughts or wanting to harm yourself in any way?   YES/NO

....

Suicide in depression

It is estimated that 90% of people who commit or attempt suicide suffer from an underlying mental illness like severe depression, bipolar disorder, psychosis, schizophrenia, anxiety disorders, borderline personality disorders, anorexia and substance abuse at the time of their death. Although depression is more common in women than men, its most dramatic outcome which is death by suicide is more common in men. A majority of men who die from suicide have not asked for help. As mentioned previously, men often suffer from depression in silence because they find it hard to open up emotionally and therefore don't seek help in time or at all. Most of them will resort to use of alcohol, drugs and self-harming to numb their emotional pain. A suicide attempt is often a cry for help that should never be overlooked, as at this overwhelmingly rock- bottom point the sufferer feels hopeless, defeated and therefore feels no point in carrying on, ending it all seeming the only way out for them to stop the pain and suffering. Anyone who expresses suicidal thoughts or intentions should be taken seriously as this is a sign that something is terribly wrong.

Men with suicidal tendencies are also more likely to be affected by risk factors like working in jobs where fire arms are accessible for instance in the armed forces where they are exposed to extreme violence and with greater risks of Post Traumatic Stress Disorder (PTSD). Many men commit suicide in prisons too due to severe violence and bullying. Unemployment also has a negative knock on effect on men than women. There are three times more men than women committing suicide and statistics in

Britain suggest that suicide is the biggest killer of men between 20 and 49, more than road accidents, cancer and coronary heart disease. A majority of the men who commit suicide have suffered from a mental illness.

Medication for depression

Although medication is the most commonly used and effective way to relieve the symptoms of depression, other therapies and approaches work well alongside. Antidepressants are tablets that treat the symptoms of depression. These have to be prescribed by the doctor mainly for moderate or severe depression. There are thirty different kinds of antidepressants which all work in different ways. Therefore a good understanding of the medication you're taking is crucial as it will increase your knowledge, confidence and trust in the treatment and also diminish any anxieties you may have about medication. In cases of side effects or if you're concerned that the medication isn't working for you, you should consult your doctor immediately so that they can monitor your progress or change your medication. The British National Formulary which provides expert advice on the use of medicines recommends that people should keep taking the effective dose for their depression for at least six months after the depression has lifted. If you stop treatment early on, the depression is more likely to return.

Types of antidepressants

Selective Serotonin Reuptake Inhibitors (SSRIs)- These antidepressant drugs have been in use for 30 years. They work by blocking the re-uptake of serotonin into the nerve cell that released it, which prolongs action in the brain. They are also used to treat other mental disorders like anxiety disorder, Obsessive Compulsive Disorder(OCD), Bulimia Nervosa. Examples are Citalopram, Ecitalopram, Fluoxetine, Fluvoxamine, Paroxetine, Sertraline. The side effects caused by SSRIs are generally easier to cope with than those of other types of antidepressants thus SSRIs are the most commonly prescribed type of antidepressant in the United Kingdom. They are more suitable for the elderly, physically ill or those at high risk of suicide.

Common side effects include;

o Nausea
o Insomnia
o Dizziness
o Weight gain or loss
o Sweating
o Decreased alertness

Serotonin and Noradrenaline Reuptake Inhibitors (SNRIs)- These are one of the newer antidepressant drugs and are very similar in action to SSRIs but they act on noradrenaline as well as serotonin. These drugs are better at targeting the brain chemicals which affect mood without causing unwanted side effects, they are sometimes preferred for treatment of severe depression and anxiety. Examples are Cymbalta, Effexor, Pristiq, Fetzima, Khedezla.

Side effects are;

- o Nausea
- o Diarrhoea
- o Dizziness
- o Agitation
- o Sexual dysfunction
- o Excessive sweating
- o Dry mouth

Tricyclic antidepressants- These are one of the oldest type of antidepressants, the are effective in the treatment of depression because they prevent the re-uptake of the able menoamine, neurotransmitters, noradrenaline and serotonin. These drugs tend to cause more unpleasant side effects compared to the other type of antidepressants, so are not suitable for the elderly, physically ill or those at a high risk of committing suicide. Examples are Anafranil, Tofranil, Elavil, Silenor, Adapin, Pamelor, Vivactil, Vanatrip, Amoxapine, Amitriptyline, Doxepin, Desipramine, Imipramine.

Side effects;

- o Tooth decay
- o Decreased alertness
- o Dry mouth
- o Constipation
- o Drowsiness
- o Urinary retention
- o Weight gain due to increased appetite

Monoamine Oxidase Inhibitors (MAOIs)- These work by making it harder for an enzyme monoamine oxidase that breaks down nonadrenaline and serotonin to do its job causing these chemicals to stay active in the body for longer. People taking MAOIs should follow a strict diet as these drugs react to certain foods. Examples are Marplan, Nardil, Parnate, Emsam, Zelapar, Eldepryl.

Side effects;
- o Decreased alertness
- o Serotonin syndrome
- o Diabetes
- o Suicidal feelings
- o Neuroleptic malignant syndrome
- o Syndrome of Inappropriate Antidiuretic Hormone

Cognitive Behavioural Therapy (CBT)

Cognitive refers to thought and thinking and behavioural means action taken and the things we do. CBT is a therapy about looking at the way you think and how your thoughts affect the way you feel and act. CBT is a common type of mental health counselling which helps a depressed person to be aware of their thoughts so that they can view challenging situations more clearly and respond to them in a more effective way. This helps the individual to alter their thought pattern from negative to positive and also help resolve their distress and increase their ability to solve problems and make decisions for themselves.

CBT is mostly carried out on a one to one basis and can also be offered in small groups. It will generally involve 16-20 sessions over a period of 3-4 months with a trained therapist. The therapist's role in CBT is to listen, learn and help the depressed person to understand their current thought patterns. CBT aims to deal with the here and now such as your current thoughts and behaviour affecting you in the now. CBT does not dwell in the past but only to find solutions to help you to change your current thoughts and behaviours so you are better equipped to deal with them in the now and in the future.

CBT is hard work and requires a great deal of commitment and persistence for you to be able to improve your situation with the help of your therapist. Although CBT has been shown to be an effective way of treating depression and other mental illnesses, it is also not suitable for everyone. It's been often criticised for only addressing current problems and not addressing underlying causes or the rest of the problem. It is also not suitable for people with complex mental health needs or learning difficulties due to its structured nature. People with mild depression will often respond well to talking about their problems and would therefore benefit immensely from CBT.

Negative thinking in depression

In many cases depression is the result of habitual negative thoughts called cognitive distortions. This is a term used in psychology to describe irrational inflated thoughts or beliefs that distort a person's perception of reality usually in a negative way. Cognitive distortions come unprompted and always seem true and believable to the thinker, often associated with feeling down or under a dark cloud and can take a serious toll on one's mental health. They include;

1. Catastrophizing: Assuming the worst outcomes of situations. "Why bother I will fail".

2. Mind reading: Assuming that you know what people think about you. "I can sense they don't like me from the way they look at me".

3. Personalising: Taking things personally resulting into self-blame. "The relationship failed because of me".

4. Should statements: "I should have done things differently", "They should have told me earlier".

5. Fortune telling: Predicting the future negatively. "I know that I will fail the interview".

6. Overgeneralization: Perceiving a wide pattern of negatives basing it on a single event. "I am never successful at anything".

7. Labelling: Labelling yourself and other people based on one experience or event. "She is a horrible person", " I am useless at everything".

8. Blaming: Blaming someone or something for your faults.

9. Dismissing the positives: Failing to recognize the good things in your life or the good things about other people. "It's his job to do that" "My achievements are nothing they don't account for anything".

10. Black and white thinking: Seeing everything in terms of either/or, winner/loser and nothing in between. "It was a complete waste of time".

11. Magnifying: Blowing things out of proportion.

12. Emotional reasoning: letting your feelings guide your interpretation of reality." I feel stressed and frustrated about my work, its not working for me, I'm resigning".

13. What ifs: Asking questions frequently of what ifs. " What if I fail at it?", "What if they don't like me?"

14. Judgement focus: Evaluating yourself, others and events without accepting or understanding basing your judgement on a personal whim aiming to find shortfalls. "I don't do well enough", "He always performs better than me."

The Benefits of CBT

o You learn to control your thinking, stopping unwanted negative thoughts.

o You become more rational in your thinking and behaviour.
o You will have more self-belief as you're more in control of your thoughts.
o You become more calmer and relaxed.
o You expect better outcomes out of situations as your thoughts are more rational and positive.

Mindful Based Cognitive Therapy (MBCT)

MBCT is another form of therapy which combines ideas of cognitive therapy with meditative practices based on the mindful concept of paying attention to the present moment without judging or worrying about what the future holds. MBCT promotes increased awareness and acceptance of thoughts and feelings.

Unlike CBT it does not try to change the content of negative thinking but rather encourages the sufferer to change their relationship with their thinking and feelings hence breaking the pattern of negative thinking.

Interpersonal Psychotherapy (ITP)

ITP is a time limited short term and effective therapy that is designed to address the needs of the depressed person. ITP focuses on conflict with another person, life events that affect how you feel about yourself and others, grief, loss, broken relationships, difficulty in starting and keeping relationships going. According to ITP, depression has the following symptoms; the symptoms of your depression, symptoms of your social and interpersonal life and symptoms of your personality and its goal is to understand, alleviate and prevent symptoms of depression. Studies have shown that ITP which addresses interpersonal issues may be as effective as short term treatment with antidepressants for mild to moderate depression.

Dynamic Interpersonal Therapy (DIT)

DIT is a time limited talking therapy that focuses mainly on relationship problems. Ideally when a person is able to deal with a relationship problem more efficiently, their psychological symptoms often improve. DIT is effective in treating depression, emotional and relationship problems by exploring difficult issues in the past that are continuing to affect the way a person may feel and behave in the present. The therapist will talk to you about your depression as well as current and past relationships so that they can understand how they are connected.

In depression, DIT aims to help the sufferer to recognise specific relationship patterns and to make changes in their relationship. During therapy, the therapist will encourage you to reflect on how you think and feel, thus helping you to manage your present interpersonal problems so that you can relieve your symptoms of distress and understand yourself and others and also help you to find ways of coping with the problems you're facing in your relationships.

Psychodynamic Therapy

Psychodynamic therapy is another form of talking therapy used to treat depression. This form of therapy is designed to help patients to explore the full range of their emotions, including the feelings they may not be aware of. By awakening the subconscious elements of their present experience, psychodynamic therapy helps the sufferer to understand how their behaviour and mood are affected by the unresolved issues and subconscious feelings. Psychodynamic sessions are usually once a week and during therapy the person will be encouraged by the therapist to talk freely about whatever they have on their mind and as they do this, the patterns of behaviour and feelings that are rooted in past experiences and unrecognised feelings will surface.

Couple Therapy and Family Therapy

Depression not only affects the person who is depressed, but it also affects the lives of people around them, for example in a couple or family. Therefore couple or family therapy is very important as it helps everyone to open up about how they feel and think and for relationships to be explored. They can also get advice and guidance, improve communication, resolve conflicts, learn skills about how to deepen family connections and how to get through difficult times as a unit either a couple or family. It will also help family members to understand the symptoms of depression and how to effectively deal with them. Having the support of family around facilitates recovery for a depressed person, therefore this form of therapy is important alongside other treatments.

****

Ch. 9

Alternative and Complementary Therapies for Depression

Massage Therapy:

Massage is a therapy that is very relaxing for a vast majority of people. It can be provided by physiotherapists, occupational therapists, massage therapists, a loved one can also give a simple massage which can be as effective and relaxing. Massage therapy can be beneficial for relaxing both body and mind, improving mood, relieving tension in muscles and increasing blood flow. If used alongside other treatments, it can help manage depression and associated symptoms such as back pain, muscle aches, fatigue, sleeping problems and stress reduction. Examples of massages are; deep tissue massage, shiatsu, hot stone massage, Swedish massage and reflexology.

Reflexology:

Reflexology is similar to massage, it has gained a lot of popularity recent in times and has proved to be effective in relieving symptoms of depression. Reflexology is performed by applying specific techniques with the hands and fingers to specific areas of the feet and massaging or applying pressure to these specific points. The reflexologist is able to release any blocked energy flow that may be responsible for causing your pain. In depressed people reflexology will;

- o Release feel good hormones- Induce state of calm and relaxation
- o Increase blood flow in the body
- o Activate the endocrine system
- o Improve sleep

Acupuncture

Acupuncture works by carefully inserting fine needles at certain sites in the body for therapeutic purposes. It is used in many NHS hospitals as well as general practices and in a number of pain clinics and hospices in the UK. Acupuncture is painless and can be very relaxing and calming. It is believed to work by stimulating the nervous system and causing the release of neuro-chemical messenger molecules, resulting in bio-chemical changes and also influencing the body's homeostatic mechanisms, hence promoting physical, mental and emotional well-being. Studies show that acupuncture can have a positive effect on depression by altering the brain's mood chemistry, increasing the production of serotonin and endorphins. Acupuncture can also reduce the physical symptoms of depression like headaches, joint pain and back pain.

Acupressure:

Acupressure is an alternative to acupuncture but without the use of needles. It is administered by the practitioner by use of fingers, palms, elbows or feet to 'acu' points by gently pressing on acupressure points on your body. Like acupuncture, acupressure releases body tension by stimulating pressure points and promoting the flow of blood in the body. Acupressure can relieve depression, stress and anxiety.

Homeopathy:

Homeopathy is a system of medicines that treat the whole person mentally and physically. It is a complimentary or alternative medicine that can be used alongside antidepressants. Homeopathy's main principles are that "like cures like" meaning that an illness caused by a substance will be cured by the same substance given in homeopathic form. Homeopathic medicines are dilute, safe and have no side effects. They are used to treat mental illnesses like depression, stress, anxiety as well as other physical illnesses.

****

Ch.10

Life Beyond Depression

You are finally on the way to recovery after being depressed for a long or short period of time and your life is slowly but steadily going back to resembling normal, however it is important that you keep an eye on depression coming back and you falling into a relapse, in fact research studies indicates that many people who recover from depression tend to experience another episode or more. Additionally, a person with a history of depression is more at risk of recurring depression.

Below are a list of some key strategies that will help you to stay on track and avoid a relapse. To avoid future relapses you will have to be able to recognise the common early signs of depression which are;

o   Losing interest in normal activities and life in general
o   Low mood and feeling down
o   Lack of energy or feeling tired
o   Feeling agitated, hopeless, irritated
o   Loss of appetite or eating more
o   Difficulty sleeping or sleeping more
o   Difficulty concentrating
o   Isolation
o   Negative irrational thinking

The main reason why people have a relapse is that when they start to feel better, they assume that they do not need any further treatment or help which is far from the truth, falling back into their old habits and lifestyles that may have contributed to their depression triggers.

It is incredibly frightening to think that you are recovering from depression and then the next thing you know is having symptoms and it striking again, it is best to put preventative measures in place and a plan to protect yourself from future relapses. The more you stick and adhere to your preventative plan, the less risk of depression resurfacing.

Staying on track

If you notice any signs of depression, the first thing for you to do is contact your doctor or psychiatrist as soon as possible for advise , support and help.

Key strategies to help you to stay on track

○ Continue to take maintenance medication, antidepressants can help treat depression as well as prevent a relapse, very often relapse is a result of premature medication withdrawal, continuing to take medication is equally as important in maintenance as in treatment especially for people who have suffered three or more episodes of depression or have chronic depression.

○ Continue with therapy sessions, which ever therapy you're having be it CBT, MCBT, IDT, ITP, o Continue with your healthy lifestyle- eat a healthy balanced diet of three meals a day with plenty of fruit and vegetables, fibre, water, nuts and seeds and a lot of fish as its rich in omega 3 and boosts brain function. Avoid any food that is high in fat, sugar and salt, cut down on caffeine, coffee, tobacco, alcohol and avoid the use of drugs. Exercising regularly will lift and boost your moods, help you stay fit and healthy both body and mind and also prevent you from relapsing. For long lasting benefits, exercise should be maintained over a long term. In cases of people with disabilities or those who are recovering from injury, surgery or any other illness, you have to avoid vigorous exercise, more so talking to a health care professional would be a good start to help you establish a healthy exercise routine that suits your needs. A healthy and restful sleep is very important too, maintain a healthy sleeping pattern as sleeping problems aggravate the symptoms of depression.

o Continue and maintain positive thinking and a positive outlook on life and situations. Inevitably you feel the way you think, so to feel good you will have to cultivate a more positive way of thinking and continue relentlessly to challenge any negative thinking with the help of CBT, CBMT, MBCT, self-hypnosis, NLP, positive affirmations, you will learn to respond more to positive thoughts thus changing your negative beliefs, attitudes, habits, behaviours and overcoming depression.

o Continue to develop and build a strong support system and healthy relationships. Family- stay connected to your family and communicate with them, although depression negatively impacts on relationships, having family members to talk to and support you is key factor in recovering from depression as well as staying on track. If you are having family therapy or couple therapy, its important that to continue with it and also spend quality time with your family, this will help strengthen your bond and renew your relationships.

o Friends- A good and strong network of friends will not only help you to get through depression but will also help you in remission and stay on track, friends will lend a listening ear, support you, advice you, and assist you with the changes you need to make in your life. All this support will give you the strength to carry on and also boost your self-worth.

o Continue your self-therapy with mind techniques like self-hypnosis, meditation, positive affirmations, relaxation techniques and NLP, these will help boost your positivity, relax you and calm your mind, help with concentration and also boost your creativity and self-esteem.

o Write a journal or diary to record your feelings, thoughts, activities, changes you've made and progress, writing has been proven to be effectively therapeutic for emotional well-being, aiding in depression recovery and personal development. Writing helps you to track your feelings and thoughts and also get them out in the open ,many people say that writing helps them to deal with their emotions, anger, agitation, frustration, thus a form of therapy in its self. Whilst being a free form of therapy it also helps you to reflect, express yourself and you actually feel better afterwards which is another bonus. You can write down your goals too, the things you want to achieve and where you want to be in a   given period of time, having ambition will power you towards achieving. You can write a diary of your daily activities and at the end of the day go through it and see what you've achieved and what you need to work on, this will keep you focussed. Writing has mental health benefits like boosting memory, it gives you a release, clears your mind, has meditative benefits like relaxing you, boosting creativity, also bottled emotions come up when you write, it eases stress and depression and more importantly helps you to spot repetitive un-healthy patterns.

o Stay motivated- There are always going to be challenges and obstacles in your way in one way or another, staying motivated will help you to initiate and maintain positive goal orientated behaviour, I believe a lot of times challenges are our best teachers because they grow us and make use stronger, however hard it is to get or stay motivated in depression, it is a big part of recovery from depression that can't be overlooked. To Stay on track, you will need to stay motivated to maintain a healthy lifestyle that incorporates a new positive thinking and outlook on life, if you lose the motivation then you will give up and fall back into relapse. Motivation will give you the purpose and desire to push on and get better. To stay motivated;

o Set realistic goals, write them down
o Be positive- think positively, surround yourself with positive people, talk positively
o Concentrate on only those things you have control over
o Live in the now
o Build a support system
o Take each day as it comes
o Keep active
o Acknowledge your achievements and reward yourself

****

Ch. 11

Stress

The nature of stress

Stress is a state of emotional strain caused by demands or pressure of everyday life. Stress can affect anyone and has become part and parcel of modern day life. Emotions caused by stress can set off a powerful physical response that will upset body and mind balance.

Negative self-talk or negative thinking patterns are also hugely responsible for a lot of stress in life. It is up to an individual to decide whether something is stressful or not. If you decide that the situation is stressful then you are going to react negatively towards it and also how you deal with it, therefore it is important to change the way you think and view situations before you decide how you react to them.

My own point of view is that when you change your thinking, your emotions will automatically take care of themselves. When stress becomes too much, it can put your physical and mental health in danger. Stress also becomes harmful when people turn to alcohol, drug use and tobacco to try and release their stress. It is advisable to seek help in cases of extreme stress or when you feel that you can't cope anymore. However not all stress is bad, in fact stress can be good as it can spur you on to be creative, achieve success and perform your best as well as increasing your productivity.

- o Distress is negative stress
- o Eustress is positive stress

Hormones associated with stress

Cortisol- this is a steroid hormone secreted by the adrenal glands also commonly termed as "the stress hormone". Cortisol is normally released in response to acute stress as well as other events and circumstances. It is best known for its "fight or flight" response, as described below:

- o A person is faced with danger/ problem / stressor
- o The adrenal glands secrete cortisol
- o Cortisol prepares the body for fight or flight response by flooding it with glucose and by doing so supplying a sudden surge of energy to the large muscles in the body.
- o Cortisol inhibits insulin production in an attempt to prevent glucose from being stored, favouring it for immediate use.
- o Cortisol narrows the arteries while the epinephrine increases heart rate, both of which force blood to pump harder and faster.
- o The person addresses/confronts and solves the problem
- o Hormone levels return to normal.

Adrenaline- commonly known as the " flight or fight" hormone, adrenaline is also produced by the adrenal glands that triggers the body's flight or fight response. This reaction causes air passages to dilate so that it can provide muscles with the oxygen they need to fight or free from the danger. It also triggers the blood vessels to contract and direct blood towards major muscles including the heart and lungs. When adrenaline kicks in you will have a surge of energy, your heart will beat very fast, your breathing rate will rise and you will have sweaty palms.

Norepinephrine - is a hormone similar to adrenaline, its function is the same as adrenaline but it also helps to shift blood flow away from areas where it might not be very essential, towards more important areas like the muscles so you can free dangerous situations. It works by;

o Increasing the amount of oxygen to the brain enabling clear and faster thinking in problematic situations.
o Increases the heart rate- pumping more blood around the body helping muscles to work faster.
o Increasing glucose to allow muscles to work better and faster.
o Shuts down metabolic processes like digestion to allow blood and energy to go to the priority areas during stress like the brain and muscles.

Types of stress

Acute stress:

Acute stress is caused by the demands and pressures of everyday life, it lasts for a short time and it is the most commonly experienced type of stress. Acute stress can be very exciting too, for example a first date, a roller coaster ride, bungee jumping.

Chronic stress:

Chronic stress occurs when acute stress is not addressed and lasts for a very long time. This type of stress can be damaging to health, for instance by contributing to certain illnesses like cancer, heart disease, depression disorders, accidents, lung disease and others.

Causes of stress

Stress is caused by a number of factors, although it's causes will depend on an individual. It is normally triggered by life events.

Below are some of the life events that contribute;

- o Death of a loved one
- o Divorce/separation/ relationship breakdown
- o Financial difficulties- loss of income, debt
- o Chronic or terminal illness- self or loved one
- o Un-healthy lifestyle- poor diet, lack of exercise, lack of sleep, drug and alcohol abuse
- o Environmental factors- noisy neighbourhood, pollution, overcrowding, traffic noise
- o Loss of job
- o Marriage problems
- o Family problems, arguments and misunderstandings
- o Homelessness
- o Moving home

- o Getting married
- o Traumatic events- natural disasters, rape, violence, accidents, war zone experience
- o Leaving the armed forces
- o Childbirth
- o Caring for a sick loved one
- o Mental illness

Work related causes include;
- o Fear of losing job- income
- o Work overload
- o Low wages that don't constitute living expenses
- o Disinterest in job
- o Low self-esteem
- o Poor management
- o Poor communication
- o Harassment
- o Discrimination- race, age, gender, disabilities
- o Working in hazardous environment
- o Lack of respect and appreciation from management
- o Fear of giving work related public speeches or presentations
- o Lack of proper training
- o Monotony of work

Symptoms of stress

The signs and symptoms of stress often manifest in physical, cognitive, emotional and behavioural ways. Recognising these signs is important for you to be able to reduce and manage your stress levels.

Physical Symptoms:
- o Tiredness, exhaustion, low energy
- o Headaches, muscular aches and pains
- o Heart palpitations
- o Breathlessness, shallow breathing, hyperventilating
- o Diarrhoea, constipation, indigestion, heartburn
- o Lack of sleep
- o Increased or decreased appetite
- o Dry mouth
- o Nausea
- o Increased use of drugs, alcohol, tobacco

Cognitive symptoms:
- o Excess worry and inability to cope
- o Anxiety
- o Negative thinking
- o Lack of concentration
- o Memory problems
- o Poor judgement

Emotional symptoms:
- o Irritability, anger, rage, frustration, agitation
- o Moodiness
- o Depression
- o Feeling overwhelmed

Behavioural symptoms:

- o Excessive substance use- alcohol, drugs, tobacco
- o Isolation
- o Excessive eating or eating less
- o Inability to sleep or sleep too much
- o Nervousness
- o Loss of interest in activities

****

Ch. 12

Coping with Stress

Stress at work:

Work related stress is the negative reaction caused by demands and pressures at work to improve skills, increase productivity or reach deadlines. An excess of this stress can impact on your mental and physical health. However, a certain amount of stress called eustress can be helpful in pushing you to improve your performance, productivity, meet deadlines and so on.

Managing stress at work

If you're stressed at work, recognising the physical symptoms of stress early on is very important for you to be able to deal with the problems you're having before they escalate into a full blown illness. The next step should be speaking out and seeking help from your manager or boss as well as your doctor if necessary. The doctor will evaluate your situation and refer you to a specialist. In the meantime you can help yourself by;-

- o Reducing workload if possible. Don't be afraid to say no to taking on excess workload or overtime.
- o Develop or improve your working relationships with your manager and colleagues to make your work place a happier place to be for you and others.

o Eat a balanced diet which will nourish your mental and physical well-being.

o Have breaks in between and go for a stretch or relaxing walk if possible.

o Delegate your work if you're in the position to do so.

o Take holidays. Everyone is entitled to holidays and having time off work which will be good for you to recharge and build your mental and physical strength.

o Stay away from drinking too much alcohol and using drugs. They will worsen your stress symptoms.

o Think positively and see challenges as opportunities for you to grow. Any negative thinking will drain you and make you feel even worse.

Stress and financial problems

Financial difficulties affects so many people around the world, both employed and unemployed which unfortunately means that financial stress is very common. The rise in the cost of food, petrol, utility bills mortgage or rent has caused even further problems like people borrowing money that they can never afford to pay back, leading to a life of debt which causes even more stress, serious health problems, and marriage breakdowns.

Causes of financial stress

o Redundancy

o Debt problems

o Mortgage or rent increase- house repossession or eviction- homelessness o   Divorce- which is very expensive

o   Reduction in income

o   Low wages

o   Lack of jobs

o   Business failure incurring losses

o   Increase in price of utility bills, food, tuition fees

o   Death or illness- loss of earnings, funereal costs or medical bills

o   Being a single parent with only one income to live on

It is normal to be worried or anxious when you're facing financial problems, however if you feel that you can't cope and that your life has become a burden then you have to seek help or talk to someone. There is plenty of information on Gov.uk website on debt management, redundancies, dismissals and benefits. Additionally, Citizens Advise Bureau (CAB) also advises on work, debt, money, relationships, housing, benefits, law and rights, tax and education. If you want a listening ear The Samaritans are always there 24 hours to offer support.

Divorce and stress:

Going through divorce or a relationship breakdown is one of the most painful and devastating experiences to go through in life. This is a time when we are emotionally, physically and mentally drained and therefore more vulnerable to worry, anxiety, stress and depression. Divorce also brings about negative feelings, thoughts, emotions and behaviour such as resentment, guilt, anger, bitterness, frustration, self destruction and neglect which all contribute to causing stress.

However, it is not all doom and gloom. Once you accept what has happened, get to terms with it, work through your emotions and let yourself grieve, this is when things start to get better bit by bit. Every person has their own pace of healing and moving on. Divorce can also be a positive thing in that you have the chance to start a new fresh chapter in your life with a mass of lessons learned. By being single you also get to rediscover yourself again and nourish your entire being. Hence by getting fit, making new friends, starting a new course or career, giving yourself an image change, travelling the world, resurrecting neglected hobbies you can achieve all those things you have always wanted to achieve but got put on the back burner!

The most common causes of stress in divorce are;

o Broken trust in case where the marriage broke because of infidelity
o Loss of spouse, best friend, companion
o Having to tell the children and the consequences afterwards
o Telling family members and friends
o Financial worries- mortgage, rent, bills child related costs
o Challenges of single parenthood
o Low self-esteem and confidence
o Feeling guilty, angry, anxious, worry, failing
o Fear of loneliness or being single forever

Single parenthood and stress

Being a single parent is one of the most stressful experience for a person to endure. Anyone in life can become a single parent through loss of spouse, divorce, separation or through work where one partner has to work in a different country for periods of time. When one parent is "absent" and has very little or no involvement at all in the children's upbringing, all the burden and responsibilities are placed upon one parent, it can be very frustrating, draining and difficult. Never mind having to juggle work, managing finances, looking after the children, school runs, home work, activities, clubs, family, friends and hobbies which can prove hectic and almost traumatic at times.

Single parenthood is always going to be hard but it can be manageable and made less stressful, when plans are made. People have been single parents for centuries although it is becoming more and more common in recent times, in point of fact there are so many successful people who have been raised by a single parent!

The main causes of stress in single parenting are;

o   Money problems and the inability to provide for the children
o   Fear of dying and leaving the children as orphans
o   In case of illness who would look after the children
o   Illness of the children and lacking support from the absent parent
o   Child care costs- work and socialising
o   Visitation and custody problems

o Lack of communication or understanding and conflicts with the other parent

o Child support maintenance worries for the parent who has to pay it

o Lack of family support

o Lack of social life due to workload, child responsibilities and childcare problems

o Dating problems- entering new relationships

o Loneliness – no companion to share highs and lows

o Low self-esteem and self-worth for unemployed parents

Tips on reducing single parent stress

o Draw a budget for your income and expenditure and how you're going to manage it. Try and save if you can afford to do so. The CAB has got a "manage your household finances" budget tool on their website which you might find useful.

o Ask for help or accept it if it's offered from family and friends who care, being a single parent is not a failure, rather a set of circumstances, so don't see yourself as one.

o Try and build a civil relationship with your former partner or the other parent, that is if they are reasonable (a few are not no matter what you do!) and aim at communicating efficiently for the sake of the children. If it works it should be a great stress reliever and give you peace of mind, there is nothing worse than having to deal with stress of single parenthood besides fighting with your co parent.

o Take time out for yourself- you have to look after number one first which is you. Exercise regularly, learn new skills, hobbies, attend fitness classes to improve your self-esteem and confidence if you need to.

o Take time for your children, it doesn't have to be very expensive. You can go for walks,, running, cycling, swimming, read books together, go to the movies, gardening, cooking, the list is endless, it's the quality of the time that you spend with them that matters not quantity!

o Have a routine for the children and set boundaries as well as maintaining discipline. A routine for children is reassuring and shows them that you're in charge.

o If you wish, join a single parent group in your local area or online for support from other single parents in the same situation as you.

o Stay positive.

Bereavement and stress:

We all lose someone we love at some point in our lives and know first hand how devastating going through this loss is. Bereavement affects people in different ways but for some people losing a loved one can be overwhelming, unbearable and incredibly stressful. The different stages of grief are;

1-Shock and denial- at this stage you will react to the loss which you may deny or pretend it hasn't happened, in other words you may refuse to take the news in.

2-Pain and guilt- here the pain will come after the shock wears off. In some cases this is accompanied by guilt about the things that you did or shouldn't have done.

3-Anger and bargaining- looking for blame, either yourself or other people, or even blaming your beloved one for dying, with a lot of questions like "why me"? "Why not them"? "Why now"? It's at this stage of bereavement that so many people question and lose their faith in their spiritual beliefs or fall out with friends, spouses and family members.

4-Depression- At this stage of bereavement, your loss sinks in and it becomes real that your beloved is no more that you may go into isolation to reflect on life as a whole.

5-Acceptance- this is a stage when you are ready to move on with your life without your loved one, You start making plans for the future and allowing yourself to be happy again. Having said that, grief is a personal and harrowing experience, everyone has their own way of dealing with it, therefore no one should ever be or feel hurried to get through it. For some people it takes a few months yet for others several years. In this acceptance stage it's easier to cope with the symptoms of stress that are caused by grief, but if you feel under a constant dark cloud and feel that coping with life has become a daily challenge for you, this is when you have to seek help from your doctor. The charity Cruse has bereavement counsellors at hand who are always there to listen, support and give practical help. The causes of bereavement stress are;

o   Inability to cope without the deceased.
o   Financial worries in case where the deceased was the income provider.
o   Guilt, anger, frustration, sadness, loneliness
o   Funeral arrangements and costs.
o   Lack of sleep
o   Fear of the unknown and not being in control of events like death.

Tips on reducing bereavement stress

o   Face the reality of your loss, the sooner the better- if you postpone grief it will sooner or later catch up with you no matter what, and you will still have to deal with it.
o   Work through the painful memories and allow yourself to experience the emotions, let it out, cry for days if you must, you can also talk about grief if you feel it's right for you.
o   You are only human so you will have bad days, allow yourself to be sad as it's all part of the healing process.
o   Keep active- this will lift your moods and relieve your stress, take your mind off your grief and also boost your sleep.
o   Eat well for your well-being, your loved one has passed but you're still alive so your well-being is important.

o Seek help and support and reach out to others who are struggling with loss. Your support will help them and also make you feel good about yourself.

o Be patient with yourself, move at your own pace. Grief takes time, has no time line, don't be compelled to rush it because other people expect you to do so. It's your grief so grieve your way, whatever feels right for you is the right way and soon you will heal and learn to live with your loss.

Chronic illness and stress

Chronic illness means a condition or disease that is persistent. Long term examples are HIV, asthma, diabetes, crohn's disease, CAD, epilepsy, multiple sclerosis, bipolar mood disease etc. Chronic illness can be very painful thereby causing a lot stress. It is estimated that up to one third of people with a serious medical condition have symptoms of depression. Chronic illness can affect the sufferer in many ways and bring about many changes in lifestyle, a number of people with chronic illness will give up jobs, careers, activities and hobbies they used to enjoy because of the pain and reduced mobility which in turn affects their confidence accompanied by negative feelings, sadness, anger, frustration, hopelessness all of which build up masses of stress which in some cases escalates into depression.

Some of the causes of stress in chronic illness are;

o Fear of having a long-term life threatening illness
o Pain and discomfort

o   Adjusting to new changes
o   Financial worries
o   Minimised independence and having to rely on other
o   Loss of mobility
o   Giving up work, activities, hobbies
o   Feelings of sadness, isolation, confusion, frustration, loneliness, anger
o   Low self-worth

Traumatic events and stress

Post Traumatic Stress Disorder (PTSD) is a serious potentially debilitating condition that occurs in people who have experienced or witnessed frightening or distressing events, for example natural disasters like tsunamis, earth quakes, floods, hurricanes, tornadoes and also traumatic events like terrorist incidents, war, accidents, sudden death of a loved one, violent personal assaults like rape, robbery and being held hostage.

PTSD can be developed immediately after someone experiences the traumatic event or it can occur weeks, months or even years later. PTSD is always characterized by flashbacks, nightmares, confusing feelings, intrusive thoughts and images as well as physical symptoms like aches and pains, excess sweating, trembling, heart palpitations, nausea, headaches and extreme emotional distress when reminded of the event. It's important to get help as soon as possible or the symptoms will become intense and the stress or depression will be prolonged.

****

Ch.13

How Stress Affects The Body

There is a powerful connection between your mind and body. Numerous studies have indicated that nothing holds more power on the body than the mind. Beliefs, habits, attitudes and their effects have an impact on the body as they do on the mind. So it is the case that whatever affects the mind will in return affect the body. Stress affects the human body in various ways:

The Respiratory System :

When you are under stress your breathing tends to be laboured and shallow, likewise when you're relaxed you breath more deeply through your diaphragm. Deep breathing techniques, relaxation techniques, meditation, exercise when practiced can all be of great use in relieving stress symptoms.

The Muscular System:

When you're stressed, the muscles tense up which is the body's way to prevent injury and also guard against pain. The muscles that are mainly affected by stress are the shoulder muscles, muscles of the neck and jaw, the breathing muscles and the diaphragm. If muscles remain tense for long periods of time they can be quite painful that's why progressive muscle relaxation techniques, massage and exercise all play an important role in relaxing your muscles.

The Cardiovascular System:

Stress that occurs over short periods of time (acute stress) brings about an increase in hormones such as adrenaline, noradrenaline, cortisol, increasing heart rate, raising blood pressure and dilating blood vessels. Meanwhile chronic stress over a long period of time can cause damage to the cardiovascular system as a result of the constant increase in the heart rate, blood pressure and heightened levels of stress hormones. This can also ultimately increase the risk of hypertension, heart attacks or stroke.

The Endocrine System:

For the body to be able to cope with stress, the adrenal glands found in the endocrine system have to make more cortisol and if they do not respond, it can be life threatening.

The Digestive System:

When you're stressed you may find that you're eating a lot more than normal or increasing your alcohol consumption and smoking. Stress can cause your oesophagus to go into spasms increasing acid in your stomach making you feel hungry and also causing indigestion. Additionally, stress affects digestion and how quickly food travels though your body.

The Nervous System:

The Sympathetic Nervous System (SNS) is responsible for creating the "fight or flight" response, then the body is under stress threat. This prepares it to either fight whatever threat it has encountered or flee.

The Female Reproductive System:

Stress in young girls and women may cause irregular or missed periods. When a woman is experiencing high levels of stress, the adrenal glands produce more cortisol in response, this excess cortisol influences the amount of oestrogen and progesterone produced, which in turn impacts on the menstrual cycle. Stress can also worsen premenstrual syndrome symptoms which are bloating, cramping, abdominal pain, fluid retention, anger, agitation and mood swings. Furthermore, when women reach the menopause stage in their lives, hormone levels decline rapidly.

The Male Reproductive System:

Chronic stress can affect testosterone production, sperm production, maturation and cause erectile dysfunction or impotence. Excess stress can also affect libido in men.

Stress and lifestyle

It is important that you review your lifestyle- habits and behaviours that may be causing or contributing to your stress. These include diet, your activity levels, alcohol intake, drug use, sleeping pattern, smoking habits, caffeine consumption.

Diet:

It is important to note that whatever you put into your body contributes immensely to its maintenance and nourishment. The food you eat will have a diverse effect on your mental and physical health, eating the right food will not only boost your mental and emotional health, but it will also help you to lose weight and stay healthy. Stress and diet are linked therefore people on a poor diet are more likely to be affected by stress than people on a healthy diet. It's very common for people who are stressed to eat more food high in sugar, fat and salt or indulge in emotional eating so its imperative to keep an eye on what you eat. A balanced diet should comprise three meals a day with the right amount of calories and portions and should contain:

- o Carbohydrates
- o Proteins
- o Fats
- o Vitamins and minerals
- o Plenty of fruit and vegetables
- o Plenty of water
- o Fibre or roughage

Obsessing about what you eat and your diet will worsen your stress. If you over-eat you will feel guilty afterwards which will increase your stress. In addition, if you're fixated on dieting and lose some weight during the time you're on the diet but then put all back on this will also trigger stress. Diets don't always work, they are a quick fix not a long term measure for successful weight loss therefore should be avoided at all costs. Diets are nutritionally unbalanced, they slow your metabolism down, further more when you're on a diet you miss out on some groups of foods and nutrients. In short, diets will leave you emotionally unbalanced, confused and even more stressed. Foods high in sugar, salts and fats are all well known for worsening symptoms of stress and therefore their consumption should be minimised or avoided.

Exercise:

Exercise is another simple and natural way to relieve stress. When you exercise or take part in any physical activity, feel-good hormones known as endorphins are released which help relieve stress. Regular activity will increase your fitness levels and boost your confidence as you will begin to feel good about yourself. It will improve your quality of sleep and enhance positivity too.

Sleeping Pattern:

Sleep and rest are among the essentials of human survival, fitness and well-being. When we sleep, we restore brain chemicals and rest the body. Worries, anxiety and the pressures of daily life contribute a great deal to stress. The ability to have a restful sleep helps the body to recover so it can function properly. Adopting new habits, some of which are outlined below, will help boost your sleep.

- o Eat a balanced diet
- o Keep active
- o Establish a bedtime routine
- o Have a relaxation routine before you wind down
- o Make your bedroom comfortable and relaxed to sleep in
- o Don't take work to bed
- o Avoid napping during the day

- o Don't put off sleeping to do other things- sleeping should be among your priorities
- o Consume alcohol in moderation
- o Don't smoke or drink caffeine prior to sleep

Alcohol consumption:

Excess use of alcohol can lead to a number of detrimental mental, physical and psychological effects. People who are stressed tend to drink more to drown their sorrows. A number of research studies suggest that alcohol increases stress by stimulating production of the same hormones the body produces when under stress which increases stress rather than decreasing it. Some of the conditions linked to chronic heavy drinking are; anaemia, high blood pressure, coronary heart disease, liver disease(cirrhosis) depression, seizures, nerve damage, pancreatitis, impaired memory and damaged self-esteem.

Caffeine consumption:

Caffeine is a drug that in large amounts stimulates the nervous system for up to24 hours. It is mainly found in tea, coffee, hot chocolate and energy drinks. Among the benefits of caffeine are that it gives you energy boost and increases levels of alertness. However when consumed excessively it can increase stress, cause fatigue, increasing blood pressure and inflating heart rate.

Smoking habits:

Evidence shows that smoking causes and increases stress rather than reduce it, Many people smoke when they are experiencing stress. Although there is a feeling that smoking can help a person to relax in actual fact the nicotine in cigarettes increases anxiety and tension hence increasing stress. Nicotine gives you a brief high or hit from dopamine as well as being very dangerous, lethal and highly addictive. Nicotine increases heart rate and therefore can cause heart problems, stroke, CHD, PVD, chronic bronchitis, emphysema, pneumonia, and cancers of the lungs, oesophagus, kidney, liver, voice box, stomach, bladder, mouth, throat, and pancreas. In cases of people who are suffering from extreme stress, quitting would provide them with an opportunity to get rid of stress as well as preventing all the afore mentioned smoking related illnesses.

Drug use:

As with smoking and alcohol consumption, people turn to drugs to escape the anxieties that are causing stress. Researchers have long recognised the correlation between stress and drug use especially in cases of a relapse in drug use. Drugs such as cocaine and heroine are often used to relieve stress but the reality is that drug abuse affects your brain in much the same way that stress does. Drug use is dangerous because it is addictive and can easily lead to death, financial problems, health risks, loss of job, home, family and friends. Many addicts find it hard to stop using or even recognising that they have a problem mistaking their addiction as a habit which they can easily give up when they choose to, which is not always the case. However with the right treatment and support addiction can be beaten but the first step is to recognise it, accept that you have a problem and then seek the help you need.

Ch. 14

Stress and the Mind

Although a certain amount of stress can be good, stress that persists for a long time will start to affect brain function, cognitive functioning and impairment of memory. Stressful events promote the release of adrenaline in the blood which sends a lot of energy to the brain for quick action. The adrenaline levels go back to normal after some time, but in some serious cases, the body releases glucocorticoids a type of steroidal hormone that directly reaches the hippocampus.

An imbalance of sympathetic and parasympathetic hormones arising due to chronic stress destroy the cells of the hippocampus region of the brain which affect logical thinking and also contribute to depression. Stress related disorders result from abnormal responses to prolonged anxiety. Acute stress disorder, also classified as anxiety disorder is caused by overwhelming traumatic events or sudden changes in personal circumstances.

Understanding how your mind contributes to generating stress will help you to deal with external and internal pressures in a better and healthier way.

Self-hypnosis in stress relief

Hypnosis in stress relief can be performed by a hypnotherapist or done individually as self-hypnosis and has proven to be very effective in helping with;

- o Relaxation
- o Deep breathing
- o Providing new coping mechanisms
- o Relieve anxiety
- o Induce calmness and relieving panic

Stress relief self-hypnosis script

I will make myself as comfortable as I can ...... take a nice deep breath ...... close my eyes and begin to relax ...... just thinking about relaxing every muscle in my body ..... from the top of my head to the tips of my toes ...... As I begin to focus attention on my breathing ...... my awareness of everything around me will decrease ..... I let all the muscles in my face, around my eyes and jaw relax ...... and as I concentrate on relaxing and releasing all tension in this area I feel the tension leaving my body ...... I continue to breath in and out relaxing the muscles in my neck and shoulders ...... feeling the tenseness and then releasing and relaxing these muscles ...... continuing to feel lighter and lighter ..... I start relaxing my back muscles while I breath in and out .... and I notice that with each breath I take in and out I feel even more relaxed .... I relax my stomach and thigh muscles ...... and move on to the muscles in my legs ..... and then to the tips of my toes tensing them and releasing them .... I am feeling a mass of calmness engulfing all my body .... floating higher and higher into a deeper level of relaxation .... I am now completely relaxed .... more relaxed than I have ever felt before .... completely relaxed from the top of my head to my toes .... my mind is calm and relaxed ...... drifting and floating ...... as I experience this beautiful feeling of peace and calm...... I will let go completely .... drifting, relaxing and drifting .....

Now that I am completely relaxed ...... I am imagining myself in my special place ...... feeling relaxed more deeply relaxed than I have ever felt before .... I begin to concentrate on how my body is feeling ..... how my mind is feeling .... no one wants anything from me ....   this time its just me ...... now I give myself permission completely to let go of all worry and tension ...... to let it happen .... my body feels free ...... and lighter ...... my muscles feel released ....yet stronger .... I concentrate on my muscles that have tendency to feel tense ....feeling how they are at the moment ...... I feel at peace .... deeply relaxed and ready to deal with the day more effectively .... I notice that my breathing is slower .... stable .... deeper .... this feeling is so much better .... I am so much more at peace and relaxed .... as I continue to relax .... I feel completely relaxed and

totally stress free .... the constant interfering noise has left ......
that irritating noise has left my mind there is no longer room for
it .... my mind is free .... and for a while I am going to let it
drift ...... and drift .... let it think of gentle peaceful things ....
positive things ...... good times that I have had in the past ......
happy times .... lovely times that I wish to have in again the
future .... no unpleasant thoughts are allowed in my mind
when I am in this state and if they try .... I will easily push
them away .... in this relaxed and calm state of my mind ......
my subconscious will accept all the suggestions and new ways of
dealing with stress ...... my subconscious hears everything and
always pays attention ..... and it is my subconscious mind that I
am talking to right now ....Now as my mind is at peace my
body is at peace too .... I let go of myself and become open to
the changes that I want to make in my life from this day forward
..... with my powerful imagination I can see and feel just how I
want my life to be .... I know now how important it is to spend
time relaxing .... how much clearer everything becomes .....how
much free ..... how much motivated I can feel and above all how
much better I feel now that I have found this special way of
letting the stress go out of my life .... more and more I am

realising that I have control over the stress and how I feel .... I can let it go .... I can let it go .... I have made my body and mind feel like this ...... and I can do it again and again ..... and be so much less stressed .... less confused and so very much more in control .... more at ease ...... From this moment on I will be calm when dealing with stressful situations ...... I will deal with them in a positive way ....these suggestions will become stronger with each day and be part of me ...... the things that cause stress and worry in my life won't trouble me any more ...... because I have new ways to deal with them ..... regardless of what is going on around me I will stay calm ...... because of this my body will be tense free ...... my mind will be clearer ...... I'm able to cope with confidence and calmness because I'm in control of how I think, feel and act ...... and with each day that passes I feel more whole and stronger ...... and these suggestions and new ideas will grow stronger and stronger with each day that passes ...... and it will be very natural for me to feel calm and relaxed in any situation ....Now that I have learnt how to relax I can appreciate how good it feels and how much my body and mind need to experience this feeling and how very much better everything feels when I have reached this inner feeling of calm

......I will enjoy my special place for another moment .....
experience it ..... drift and float ..... I am feeling calm and relaxed
...... In a few minutes I will come back to awareness ...... I will
count from one to ten .... and as I count from one to ten I will
begin to come back to full awareness ..... I will come back feeling
calm and relaxed ....

1.................... Begin to come back

2 ....Feeling relaxed

3 ....Calm and peaceful

4 ....Feeling relaxed

5 ....I am aware of the normal surroundings now

6 ....I begin to open my eyes now

7 .... I open my eyes and come back feeling wonderful

****

Ch.15

Relaxation Techniques in Stress Relief

Relaxation techniques can reduce stress symptoms and are also a great way to help with stress management. When the muscles in your body relax, your mind relaxes too, and your heart rate and pressure decrease. Relaxation techniques can help you cope with life stresses and other stress related illnesses and disorders. Learning relaxation techniques is easy and comes at no price yet is beneficial to improving your health. To practice this simple technique you will need to find a quiet place. You will find that you will gain more confidence and also become more aware of muscle tension in your body when you're under stress. Below are some of the different relaxation techniques.

1. Autogenic relaxation- In this type of relaxation, a person imagines that they are calm and relaxed like in self-hypnosis.
2. Visualization or Imagery-This form of relaxation technique also induces relaxation and improves physical and mental well-being. All senses are used in this form of relaxation.
3. Meditation
4. Yoga
5. Massage
6. Tai chi

7. Exercise
8. Deep breathing
9. Music and art therapy

All of these relaxation techniques help to relax the body and mind and are therefore useful in relieving stress and its symptoms. The benefits of relaxation in reducing stress symptoms are;

o Slows the heart rate
o Lowers blood pressure
o Slows breathing rate
o Reduces muscle tension
o Relieves pain
o Reduces activity of stress hormones
o Increases blood flow to major muscles
o Improves concentration
o Improves mood
o Reduces fatigue, anger, agitation
o Boosts confidence
o Boosts positivity

PMR technique

o Find a quiet place ......
o Sit comfortably with a straight back with both feet on the floor, rest your arms on your lap .....
o Breath in through your nose into your abdomen slowly and relax ......

o Close your eyes and direct your attention to your face, around your eyes, concentrate on the muscles here tense them and feel their tightness and then relax them ...... feeling very relaxed letting all the tenseness fade away .....- Now move to your jaw and neck, there is always a lot of tension in this area ...... hold for five seconds and then relax these muscles and feel them loosen up and relax ......

o Move on to the muscles in your shoulders ...... tense them and release ...... feel them relax .....

o Bring your focus to your hands ..... tense the muscles in your hands and hold .....concentrate on the tenseness, drop them and then let them relax ......

o Now move on further to your chest and stomach muscles, tense and tighten them ...... hold for 5 seconds and relax them .....

o Now breath in and fill your lungs completely ...... and then breath out deeply through your abdomen and direct your attention to your back ..... tense it ..... and relax ..... letting all the tension dissolve away .....

o Tighten your thigh and buttock muscles .... relax them and feel the difference ..... now tense your legs and curl your toes experiencing the tension ..... release and relax ...

o As you carry on you will feel a deep relaxation sweeping through your entire body ..... continuing to breath in and out gently and deeply ...... relaxing even more and letting go of any residue of aches and pains in your body ......

****

Ch. 16

Mindfulness in Stress Relief

_____

Mindfulness is the awareness that derives from paying attention to the now and living in the present moment. It doesn't help that we live in a busy frantic world with goals to accomplish, ever present expectations from ourselves and others, deadlines, routines, targets, responsibilities and so on.

This is where mindfulness comes into play, mindfulness relaxes the mind just as PMR relaxes the body. The mindfulness approach to stress works in a way that it helps to calm the mind down so that it's easier to deal with situations and be able to experience them without reacting negatively, as well as being able to go through difficult events other than avoiding them. Whether you're going through stress at work, divorce, bereavement, financial problems, illness or any other situation, mindfulness will help you to go through all the feelings and emotions, good or bad.

Mindfulness will catapult you from worrying about the future and what will happen or may not happen, by being mindful you live in the present and experience life fully, because its what counts. Mindfulness is also an effective meditative tool that can help regulate breathing, stop constant rambling thoughts going through your mind and also change the way you view yourself. When you're mindful, you're more calmer and relaxed which helps to relieve stress, anxiety and worry. The benefits of mindfulness include;

- o It relieves stress
- o Lowers blood pressure
- o Reduces chronic pain
- o Alleviates gastro intestinal problems
- o Important in psychotherapy in treatment of depression, anxiety disorders, substance abuse, couples problems, Obsessive Compulsive Disorder(OCD) and eating disorders.

Mindfulness meditation for stress

- o Find a quiet place where you will be able to relax with no distractions ......
- o Get into a comfortable position, you can chose to sit down, lie down or even standing or walking, try and test all these positions to see which one works best for you .....
- o Relax into your chosen posture and start to breath in and out ..... notice your breathing ....you will begin to relax with each breath you take in .... thoughts and images will be coming in and out of your mind ..... let them come and go without judging them and continue with your breathing ...... feel the awareness that arises within your body, this will help anchor you in the present moment ...... stay mindful of any feelings and emotions that arise like anger, sadness, frustration, happiness, excitement, accept them, feel them and release them ...... also stay

mindful of any body sensations, allow yourself to feel them and let them pass

o   As your concentration grows , you will feel even more mindful and aware of your mind, body and all your senses heightened ....

o   Stay in this mindful state for as long as you want to......

****

Ch.17

Getting Help For Severe Stress

Because stress is common and affects almost everyone, it's very easy to ignore the warning signs that the stress levels have become unmanageable, consequently becoming a danger to health.

Severe stress manifests itself in various ways both physically and mentally;

o Lack of sleep due to excess worry, anxiety, and feeling burnt out.

o Weight gain or loss due to an increase or decrease in appetite.

o Use of drugs and alcohol to cope, forget or numb pain.

o Memory impairment and low concentration levels.

o Rapid heartbeat, palpitations.

o Increased blood pressure.

o Shallow breathing.

o Stomach pains, nausea, vomiting, diarrhoea, constipation due to increased blood flow and muscle contractions during times of severe stress. Don't suffer in silence seek professional help when stress and its effects have taken over your life.

o You've resorted to un-healthy ways of coping with stress for example using drugs and heavy use of alcohol.

○ You're experiencing aggressive behaviour such as angry outbursts.

Treatment of PTSD

If you're suffering from PTSD get help from your doctor as soon as possible for a referral to see a specialist. PTSD can be successfully treated even many years after the traumatic event. Whereas anti- depressants may help you feel less sad, worried or on edge, they do not treat the causes of PTSD. The main treatment for PTSD is psychotherapy which is usually recommended first. In cases of severe PSTD a combination of medication and psychotherapy will be recommended by a mental health specialist like a psychiatrist or community psychiatric nurse.

The common types of psychotherapy to treat PTSD are:

CBT, EMRT(Eye Movement Desensitisation and Reprocessing)

CBT – Trauma focused therapy that uses a range of psychological treatment techniques to help you come to terms with the trauma.

EMRT- Involves making side to side eye movements usually following the movement of your therapist's finger while recalling the traumatic event. Whilst EMRT is a new treatment, it has been found to reduce the symptoms of PSTD.

Group Therapy- sharing experiences with other people who are suffering from PSTD, group therapy helps you to manage your symptoms and understand the condition.

Counselling- there are a couple of charities which offer counselling to military and ex-military PSTD sufferers to help combat stress.

Ch.18

The Stress Management Plan

To be able to plan how to manage stress, you will need to know what triggers or causes your stress. In this case you will be able to replace these negative triggers and the physical and emotional responses to each trigger, and replace them with positive new ones as your coping mechanism.

A stress trigger and new response diary will help you to be able to document this. In this diary you will note down the date, time and place of the stressful event, what you felt emotionally, what you were thinking, what you did after the stressful event and how you felt physically. You will proceed by finding a new coping strategy for each stimuli that will help you deal with stressful episodes and keep you in the present moment.

New responses should be things that you would enjoy doing like going for a walk, listening to music, exercising, writing, shopping, deep breathing, watching a humorous programme on television, gardening, meditation, prayer, talking to a friend or family member and many more. Keeping a diary will help you understand the causes of stress in your life besides giving you an insight into how you react to stress and more importantly how you can improve the management of your stress.

Lifestyle review: Your diary should help you to identify your current stress-coping strategies. If they are not healthy ways of coping you have to look into changing these habits, for instance a poor diet and bad eating habits, no exercise, smoking habits, use of drugs, bad sleeping habits, excess alcohol use, too much caffeine consumption, watching too much television, overuse of video games and computer time, violence and aggression.

To start with, a healthy balanced lifestyle will make a big difference in boosting your health and reducing your stress. In addition, taking time out to exercise regularly will prevent and reduce stress, keeping active will burn away anger, agitation, irritability and tension that builds up in your body when you're stressed.

Furthermore your review should include a healthy sleeping plan as sleep is one of the best and natural ways to cope with stress. When you sleep your body repairs and recovers from illness. Sleep is tremendously essential for a healthy body and mind. Avoid the use of drugs, alcohol, tobacco and caffeine as it's better to deal with the root cause of your stress rather than run away from it. Substance use will only be a temporary measure to mask your problem which will damage your health in the long run and you will still have to eventually face up to your problem and deal with it at some point.

Strained or bad relationships with family, work colleagues and friends bring about overwhelming stress. Try and reach out if you can to improve these relationships, communicate regularly and allocate time for them. Relationships when not nurtured don't survive, they become strained and wither away. Socialising is a basic human need, studies suggest that those who frequently socialise may live longer than those who don't. Socialising has a strong influence upon our health and happiness not to mention playing a vital part in relieving stress and depression.

An example of a stress diary

Monday 19/03/2015

Time	Trigger	Reaction	Coping Response
7.20am	I woke up late	Panicked	Took deep breaths
9.40am	Arrived late at work	Worry, headache	Took more deep breaths
12.00pm	Boss told me off for lateness	Got angry	Went for a walk
4.20pm	Children fighting	I get angry & agitated	I counted one to ten
5.10pm	I get burnt while cooking	scream & get worked up	make a cup of tea

Positive thinking is another key element of effective stress management. People tend to think very negatively in stressful situations but if you learn to be aware of your thoughts, you will find it easy to recognise the negative ones and be able to transform them into positive ones. Thinking positively doesn't necessarily mean that you have to ignore the problems around you, it means that you deal with whatever life throws at you in a positive manner and hope for the best out of the situation. A lot of the time, challenges or problems are opportunities waiting to be discovered and explored. When you think negatively you automatically expect the worse to happen and under these circumstances you will worry, be anxious, frightened and stressed. Conversely, when you think positively you will view the stressful events as less threatening and also cope effectively with them thus reducing stress. Positive thinking can also be applied by use of positive affirmations. Affirmations are mantras or words that you can say to yourself to enforce a positive behaviour or thoughts. Affirmations are one of the easiest ways to calm down in a stressful situation. They also induce positive feelings and thoughts if used regularly. Below are a couple of positive statements to relieve stress.

Stress relief positive affirmations

- I am more relaxed than ever before
- I let go of stress with each breath I take
- I find it easy to let go and relax
- Relaxing comes natural to me
- I am calm and stress free
- My mind is calm and relaxed
- My body is calm and relaxed
- I let go of worry
- I release all tension in my body
- I am at peace with who I am
- I live in the present moment
- I think positively about life
- I am in full control of my thoughts and emotions
- I can deal with any challenges that come my way in a positive way
- I am stronger than stress
- I feel clear in my mind than ever before
- With every breath I release all anxiety and tension in my body.

o I am free of all stress, worry and tension

Generally speaking, you will have to monitor your stress management plan every now and then to ensure that you're on the right track and also make any necessary changes every now and then if need to do so.

In essence, remember that the stages involved in managing stress are;

o Recognising the symptoms of stress
o Identifying the causes
o Acting upon the causes to reduce or eliminate the symptoms.

****

Useful Addresses

British Association For Counselling and Psychotherapy(BACP)
Address: BACP House
15 St John's Business Park
Lutterworth
Leicestershire
LE17 4HB

Email: bacp@bacp.co.uk
Website: www.bacp.co.uk

Depression Alliance (Offers information on depression, treatment, recovery and self-help support groups)
Address: 20 Great Dover Street
London
SE1 4LX

Tel: 08451232320
Email: information@depressionalliance.org

Depression UK (Helps people cope with depression, offering friendly advice & support)
Address: C/O Self-Help Nottingham
Ormiston House
32-36 Pelham Street
Nottingham
NG1 2EG

Email: info@depressionuk.org

Mind (Offering help and information about mental health problems)
Address: 15-19 Broadway
Stratford
London
E15 4BQ
Tel: 02085192122
Helpline: 03001233393
Email: contact@mind.org.uk

Samaritans (A registered charity which is open 24 hours and offers support to anyone in emotional distress)
Tel: 08457909090
Email: jo@samaritans.org
Text: 07725909090

Bipolar UK (Supports people with bipolar, their families and carers)
Address: 11 Belgrave Road
London
SW1V 1RB
Tel: 02079316480
Web: www.bipolaruk.org.uk

The Mental Health Foundation (Provides information and support for anyone with mental health problems)
Website: www.mentalhealth.org.uk

Young Minds (Provides information on child and adolescent mental health, and for parents and professionals)
Address: Suite 11

Baden Place
Crosby Row
London
SE1 1YW
Website: www.youthminds.org.uk

Sane (Offers information and emotional support for people affected by mental illness, including family, friends and carers)

1st Floor
Cityside House
40 Aldler Street
London
E1 1EE
Helpline: 08457678000
Website: www.sane.org.uk

Seasonal Affective Disorder Association (Provides information, support and advice for SAD sufferers, public and health professionals)
Website: www.sada.org.uk

Suicide and Self-harm (Provides emotional support to reduce suicide)
Website: www.befrienders.org.

Association for Post Natal Illness (Provides support to mothers suffering from PND)
145 Dawes Road
Fulham

London
SW6 7EB
Email: info@apni.org
Website: http://apni.org

Citizen Advise Bureau(CAB) Provides information and advice on a number things eg healthcare, work, debt and money, relationships, housing, law and rights, discrimination, benefits, education.
Tel- England: 03444111444
Tel- Wales: 03444772020

****

References and Resources

Book References

Paul Gilbert, Overcoming Depression. A Self-Hep Guide Using Cognitive Behavioural Techniques (Robinson Publishing Ltd, 1997)

Alice Muir, Overcome Depression (Hodder & Stoughton Ltd, 2013)

Keith Souter, Understanding and Dealing with Depression (Summersdale Publishers Ltd, 2013)

Neel Burton, Growing From Depression (Acheron Press, 2010)

Josie Hardley and Carol Staudacher, Hypnosis For Change (MJF Books, 1996)

Costas Papageorgiou, Hannah Goring and Justin Haslam, Coping With Depression. A Guide to What Works For Patients, Carers and Professionals (One World Publications, 2011)

Terry Louker and Olga Gregson, Manage Your Stress for a Happier Life (The McGraw-Hill Companies, 1997)

Xandria Williams, Stress. Recognize and Resolve. How to Free Yourself from Stress Whatever Your Circumstances (Charles Letts & Co Ltd, 1993)

Resources

www.overcomedepression.co.uk/howcommondepressionis.html

www.nhs.uk..../bipolar-disorder/..../

www.mind.org.uk/..../postnataldepression/.....

www.m.webmd.com/depression/..../

www.mind.org.uk/..../antidepressants/..../

www.m.webmd.com/..../menopause-weightgain/....

www.helpguide.org/.../stress/...

www.rcpsych.ac.uk/.../copingwithstress...

www.mind.org.uk/information.../stress/

www.nhs.uk/.../stress.../reduce-stress.aspx

www.yourhormones.info/Hormones/Adrenaline.aspx

****

Index

Genetics, 23

Harassment, 91
Head injuries, 24
Headaches, 30, 33, 92
Heart disease, 24
Heroin, 24
Homeopathy, 79
Hormone changes, 14
Hypnosis, 43, 44, 45, 46, 115, 138

Illogical thinking, 31
Insomnia, 33, 40, 67
Interpersonal Psychotherapy (ITP), 74
Isolation, 81, 93

Khedezla, 68

Loss of appetite, 30, 81
Low self-esteem, 31, 33, 91, 98, 100

Male Reproductive System, 109
Mania, 18
Marijuana, 24
Marplan,, 69
Medication, 24, 25, 66
Meditation, 57, 121
Mental illness, 91
Mindful Based Cognitive Therapy (MBCT), 73
Mindful Tai-Chi, 60
Mindful yoga, 59
Mindfulness, 6, 7, 57, 61, 124, 125
Moderate depression, 12

Monoamine Oxidase Inhibitors (MAOIs, 69
Mood swings, 33
Muscular System, 107

Nardil, 69
Nausea, 67, 68, 92
Nervous System, 108
Neuro Linguistic Programming (NLP), 50
Norepinephrine, 89

Obesity, 24
Omega3, 37
Osteoporosis, 24
Over-sleeping, 40

Parnate, 69
Paroxetine,, 67
Positive thinking, 54, 131
Post Natal Depression, 20
Postpartum Depression, 15
Pre Menstrual Dysphoric Disorder, 21, 26, 33
Pregnancy, 14
Premenstrual problems, 14
Pristiq, 68
Psychodynamic Therapy, 75
Psychotic Depression, 17, 21
Puberty, 14
Reframing, 51
Relaxation techniques, 7, 53, 121
Restlessness, 33

Schizophrenia, 65
Seasonal Affective Disorder(SAD), 17

****